THE ULTIMATE GUIDE
TO
COOKING DESSERTS
THE INDIAN WAY

Prasenjeet Kumar & Sonali Kumar

To economise on costs, this book contains no photographs. However, if you wish to have a look at how the dishes should actually look like, you could either refer to the e-Book version or to the Author's website www.cookinginajiffy.com.

Edited by: Arun Kumar Ph.D.

Disclaimers

Although the Authors have made every effort to ensure that the information in this book was correct at the time of publication, the Authors do not assume and hereby disclaim any liability to any party for any loss, damage, or disruption caused by errors or omissions, whether such errors or omissions result from negligence, accident, or any other cause.

This book is not intended as a substitute for the medical advice of physicians. The reader should regularly consult a physician in matters relating to his/her health and particularly with respect to any symptoms that may require diagnosis or medical attention.

This book also assumes that the reader does not suffer from any food allergies or related medical conditions. Readers suffering from food allergies are requested to skip the recipes that contains ingredients which trigger adverse reactions in that reader or in his/her family and friends.

The spellings used in this book are British, which may look strange to our American friends, but NOT to those living in Australia, Canada, India, Ireland and, of course, the United Kingdom. This means that color is written as colour and so on. We hope that is NOT too confusing!

Table of Contents

That's what dessert means to me: a dollop of sweet love in an otherwise cold world.

—Sarah Strohmeye

Chapter 1: Desserts – Why Bother?

"I didn't know why dessert was invented or what function it was meant to perform. Raising livestock and the harvesting of grains are ancient activities, but when did humankind decide it also needed crème brulee?"

–Bill Buford

Great question. So let's start with a little history.

There is no doubt that humankind from time immemorial has loved the sweet taste as it occurred naturally on Mother Earth. If anything, our instincts taught us to eschew anything that tasted bitter and trust everything that tasted sweet.

As we learnt to grill, bake and finally cook on pots and pans, some experimentation in mixing sweet stuff like honey or fruit juice with other food products would have naturally started. But preparing a dessert, as we know it today, had to wait till sugar could be extracted from sugarcane in India. Or from beetroot in Europe.

So it was natural that Greek and Roman Symposia in 300 BC, as the classics describe, used to conclude with fresh or dried fruit and nuts ONLY.

Even in 1430, when Joan of Arc was captured by the Burgundians, she is said to have just some fruit after dinner. In Victorian England, the final course was often a "savoury," such as grilled sardines!

But the Crachit family in Charles Dickens's *A Christmas Carole*, set in the late 1830s, is described as all excited about having "the Pudding" after dinner. So it looks like sugar had reached England by that time.

The French Experience

Etymologically, the word "dessert" comes from the Old French word "*desservir*," which meant strangely "cleaning the table."

The word gained popularity in the 17th century Europe where entertaining used to be an all-evening/all-night affair. The lavish spread laid out on long dining tables used to be taken as the measure of one's social standing. And if there was one extreme stigma attached to this activity, it was to let food run short or to let anyone leave hungry.

But there was a practical problem: servants and employees had to be relieved at some point. So kitchens came up with some sweet, and prepared in advance "finishers." The easiest was honey-drenched ice that could be prepared hours in advance. Other desserts, that didn't need to be heated, and which could be prepared even the day before, soon came to be "invented."

All these innovations made it possible to let the cooks and servers get home quicker. But more importantly, these helped the host look good for serving everyone to the point of complete satiation. So what desserts did was to fill guests up to the brim and helped *"desservir,"* or "clean the table."

As the nobility also discovered, sugar, and anything sweet in general, was an appetite depressant. This meant that no one who had a dessert after a lavish meal could ever complain of being hungry.

There is also a theory that way back, before refrigeration was discovered, meats had to be heavily spiced to mask their deterioration that could border on rancidity. The sweets following the main course helped cover any such taste of the main course rather well.

Susan Pinkard in her book *A Revolution in Taste: The Rise of French Cuisine* explains how the tables of nobles contained dishes of many flavours (savoury, bitter, salt and sweet)—often with conflicting spices— as some kind of "show" of wealth. There were many gradual developments in the art and science of food preparation that included the separation of flavours, complimentary textures and a "sweet" at the very end of the meal "like the epilogue of a great book." These were often accompanied by a bitter, strong cup of coffee or tea or even cheese.

Sugar, especially cane sugar, imported as it was from distant India was an extreme luxury. Only the very rich could afford it. And so they served dessert in small amounts at the end of the meal. Having an expensive sweetened dish served at the end of the meal thus ensured it would be remembered the most.

The Health Debate

So much for the history.

Now for, aah, the eternal question.

Why should anyone in today's age and time in his right senses indulge in any calorie dense sweets, sweetmeats, desserts, *mithais* or anything that such sugary or syrupy dishes are known by anywhere in the world?

The question arises because, as the health freaks around you will tell you, all these desserts rather unnecessarily overload your system with "empty calories" and cause a sugar spike in your blood that is best avoided.

But what if you are a connoisseur of desserts, who doesn't need an occasion to celebrate? Or, if you like to "feed your soul with food that makes you feel as if heaven has descended on earth"?

Could you then tell those health freaks to take a hike and NOT feel guilty about indulging your sweet tooth for "no apparent reason?" Could you let logic take a back seat and just savour your "just desserts?"

Oh, yes now you very well can.

Apparently some latest research indicates that all such sweet stuff may (in moderation, of course) be good for your health. They in fact have some really positive effects on your health, heart, mind, and sleep.

Shocking? So read on.

Believe it or not: Sweets lessen the chances of getting a stroke

Lovers of dark chocolate will love this little piece of research.

In a study from Neurology, 37,000 Swedish men aged 45 to 79 recorded their diet over the course of 10 years. During that time, 5% experienced their first stroke.

After multivariable adjustments, those who ate the most chocolate (62.9 grams per week in this case) were found to be 17 percent less likely to suffer from a stroke than those who never had chocolates.

The researchers concluded that the flavonoids in chocolate may protect against stroke "through several biological mechanisms, including antioxidant, anti-platelet, and anti-inflammatory effects."

Another key message was that "these studies focus on the intake of dark chocolate……. Typically this is marked on the package by something containing 65 to 70% cocoa or more."

So the lesson is to check ingredient lists and either stick with cocoa powder or selectively choose your dark chocolate.

Don't you now have an excuse to eat the best-quality dark chocolate every day without feeling guilty about it?

 That's if you wish to stay fit!

Desserts make for excellent breakfast

Believe it or not, but in a study, published in Steroids, researchers at Tel Aviv University's Wolfson Medical Centre have claimed that eating cookies and cake in the morning could actually help non-diabetic obese people lose weight.

The study looked at about 200 obese adults who were put on low—calorie diets. One group ate a large 600-calorie breakfast followed by a slice of cake or doughnut or cookie, while the other was put on a

300-calorie protein-packed diet of egg whites, tuna, cheese and milk, minus any sweets.

Four months later, both groups lost about 30 pounds (about 15 kgs) per person. But, in the subsequent four months (the study's maintenance period), the high-protein group regained around 22 pounds, while the sweet-loving group continued to shed weight. Dumbfounded, researchers attributed these results to the reduced cravings, which may have made the subjects feel less hungry throughout the day.

Experts, however, advise that such studies shouldn't be taken as a license to add too much of refined sugars to your breakfast. Instead, we should try to find more natural ways to sweeten your breakfast by adding, for example, honey, agave or fruits.

Desserts lower your blood pressure

Yes, the same flavonoids in dark chocolate that lower the risk of stroke, help also reduce blood pressure. Twenty different studies reviewed by the Cochrane Collaboration established that people who ate between 3 and 100 grams of dark chocolate or cocoa powder each day lowered their blood pressure by around 2 to 3 mg Hg.

Desserts improve your love life

Research from the Smell and Taste Treatment Research Center, Chicago indicates that the zinc-packed seeds of pumpkin pie increase testosterone levels. Plus its aroma is supposed to reduce anxiety and overall cast an aphrodisiacal effect on you.

Now even if you don't particularly find the pumpkin's aroma to be a turn-on, there's no denying that this humble squash comes packed with vitamin A, iron, calcium and fibre.

In an interesting study, participants from the University of Minnesota's Joseph P. Redden and Texas A&M's Kelly L. Haw were asked to choose a snack, or dessert, and count how many times they chewed while eating. Most participants felt more satisfied when they counted their bites than when they munched mindlessly.

The researchers said in a statement that, "Dieters should focus on the quantity of unhealthy foods but not the quantity of healthy foods. Monitoring healthy foods could actually be more counterproductive to the goal of eating a healthier diet. So the secret to success is knowing when to monitor your eating."

Another conclusion was: there is no harm if you have an occasional piece of sweet but just savour it over a long period by chewing it well!

Desserts improve your mood

Who hasn't turned to a pie or an ice-cream or a box of cookies on a "bad day" to help uplift your mood?

The reason is that when you eat your favourite dessert, you are flooded with the mood-elevating hormone called Serotonin. That's what makes you feel like there's still hope left in the world!

And this feeling could be vital to your well-being.

Experts advise that constantly denying ourselves some simple pleasures (like desserts) can make us feel like we do not deserve them and can also make us resentful as human beings.

So for people for whom dessert is akin to true love, it is okay to go ahead and derive pleasure from a simple activity like eating your favourite sweets.

Desserts make loving, sharing and caring pleasurable

Even Dennis the Menace would agree.

When you taste an outstanding dessert, what do you wish to do immediately?

Of course, share it with someone you love or care for.

That way you also spread a little love around—in your family or friend circle—and reduce your calories when you're on a diet.

That's what we would call as a win-win situation.

And while theoretically you could share any good dish with people you love, desserts somehow lend themselves more easily to such sharing.

Wouldn't you agree?

Desserts make you enjoy life more

In India every happy occasion—be it a promotion, a birthday, an engagement or a wedding announcement—is celebrated with sweets.

Why? Because eating any dessert spreads cheer all around and makes your day better.

You start liking people more and feel like everything is going to be alright.

As Lea Mishell says,

"Life's short. Eat dessert first, work less and vacation MORE!!"

So how should you have your sweetmeats?

Now that we have agreed that eating dessert not only makes you healthy, but also makes you a happier and better human being, the question arises as to how we should enjoy our desserts.

Here is our two-bit advice:

1. Have your sweets in the mornings or with your breakfast as you have the whole day to use up the extra calories that are pumped in your blood stream. Some people also like to indulge their sweet tooth around 4 p.m., which is after 3-4 hours of their lunch, as it makes them perkier by giving them a serotonin boost. From this logic, having a dessert after dinner could be quite a BAD idea.

2. You don't have to be miserable to be thin and healthy. What is important is being knowledgeable about what you are eating. So if you have a choice, choose dark chocolate or nut-based desserts over the ones that only have white flour and cream. Similarly, choosing veggie based desserts like pumpkin pie or carrot halva would always be wiser. Ditto for yoghurt based desserts as they are supposed to be swimming with probiotics.

3. Exercise portion control, especially with your desserts. It is a good idea, therefore, to share your desserts generously with your friends and loved ones.

4. Mix desserts with high fibre meals. So avoid having a Tiramisu with your hamburger. But go ahead with your favourite veggie or yoghurt based dessert after your high fibre meal composed of whole grains and veggies like cabbage or broccoli.

5. Feel free to address your cravings for desserts by eating naturally sweet fruits. Try a fruit platter, therefore, 1-2 hours before your major meals like your lunch or dinner.

Chapter 2: Our Indian Sweethearts

"But I, when I undress me

Each night, upon my knees

Will ask the Lord to bless me

With apple-pie and cheese."

– Eugene Field

Sorry Mr. Field, but if you need to taste Indian desserts, you will have to forget apple and cured cheese, to start with.

You can sure have cream, milk, and fresh cottage cheese. You can use exotic spices like saffron and green cardamom. You can also use almost any grain or nuts. But just apple and cheese is not enough to please any Indian sweet tooth.

Why? Because having discovered sugar (or jaggery) from sugar cane, Indians are a little conservative about their sweetmeats. Their desserts have to be SWEET, in all senses of the term.

Their conceit may be pardoned. Because when the sweetest thing that the world knew was honey or raisins, ancient Greek writers from the days of Herodotus and Alexander were marvelling about those magical "reeds" in India that could yield a substance that would be sweeter than honey.

So it is established that sugar from sugarcane was gifted to the world by India. Even the knowhow of sugarcane cultivation and processing was spread (mostly forcibly!) to all parts of the world, from Mauritius to the Caribbean, by the British through Indian workers.

It is natural, therefore, to expect that all regions of India would have a very strong dessert making tradition. Sweets have to be offered to gods and exchanged among friends on all auspicious occasions. Any good news, even in corporate offices, would result in a clamour for some exchange of sweets much to the bewilderment and bemusement of the non-Indians around that place. Celebrating with sweets is something that comes naturally to all Indians.

India is a sub-continent of languages, cultures, and traditions that are intertwined yet independent. Each state or region has something entirely different and wonderful to offer. And there is no better way of learning about their specialities and idiosyncrasies than by savouring their delicacies.

Indian sweets, especially in Northern India, are often called *Mithai*. This is derived from the word *mitha* meaning sweet. It is interesting that some popular Indian street food desserts like *Gulab Jamuns* or *Jalebis* are deep fried (like doughnuts)! The reason could be because oil acts as some kind of preservative for such street food which, unlike home-cooked meals, doesn't normally go into a fridge.

Most of such sweetmeats, as anywhere else in the world, would be prepared by *Halwais* (professional sweet makers) in commercial outlets. So a "Home Style" tradition of making desserts should legitimately raise some eyebrows.

Why, as elsewhere, this craft of making desserts at home has still not died out in India? We asked around and learnt that the first reason is the older generation's mistrust of anything commercial. So if you want to ensure that whatever ingredients you are using are unadulterated, especially when you are making sweets for an auspicious occasion, you will make these with your very own hands.

The second, more practical reason is that this is the only way to regulate the sugar content or to enable the use of sugar substitutes in your desserts. Yes, you can use your favourite sugar-substitute, like Aspartame (Equal) or Sucralose (Splenda) in most

Indian desserts except those that require the use of a sugar syrup (like *Jalebi* or *Gulab Jamun*).

The third reason is that Indian sweets are healthier. They generally don't contain eggs; so no bad cholesterol for you. They NEVER use butter or cream or white flour in such big proportions as western cakes or pastries do. They can use veggies like cauliflower or bottle gourd or even lentils and legumes. Consequently, they have better protein and vitamin content than most western style desserts.

And finally, you still make desserts in Indian homes because YOU CAN, in a JIFFY, without special equipment or moulds, without pre-heating ovens, without waiting for hours for your stuff to bake, and so on.

So here are some of the ways in which desserts are prepared with almost everything in India:

Desserts made with rice: Yes, there are many dishes where rice is used for desserts. Apart from the familiar rice pudding, called *Kheer* in North India or *Payasam* in South India, we provide in this book the variation made with *Natun Gud* (palm jaggery), the one made with rice flakes (*Poha* or *Chiura*), and that outstanding dessert made with rice flour that the Muslims in India call *Phirni*.

In addition, we provide *Murhi Chikki* (Rice flake praline), a sweet mango-rice dish, and two South Indian desserts called *Sweet Pongal* and *Sakkarai*

Pongal, to complete our introduction to eight great Indian desserts that use rice.

Desserts made with wheat: Wheat is almost compulsory in most western desserts like pies, pastries, puffs and cakes. Indians, however, don't use wheat for making "outer coverings" only. Instead, they use wheat flour straightaway, for example, in *Aatey Ka Halwa* (Whole Wheat Flour Dessert) or *Ghola Prasad* (Whole Wheat Flour Porridge) with both deemed fit as an offering to the gods.

Then vermicelli made with wheat is used for making *Kheer* or *Sevian*, with the latter being compulsory for such Muslim festivals as *Eid*. Semolina (*Sooji*) is similarly turned in to a super-easy-to-make *Halwa* that children just love.

Wheat flour is also used for making pancake-type dishes, the most famous of which is the *Maalpua*. This dessert is compulsorily served for such festivals as Holi, the Indian festival of colours.

Use *gur* or jaggery and you can have the tasty breakfast dish—*Gur Paratha*. Fry these as spirals and you get the crispy, syrupy *Jalebis* that every sweet vendor in India could intrigue and indulge you with. Fill it with nuts and dried milk (*Khoya*) and you will have *Gujias* or *Pidukias* that are great festival dishes.

And then you have the great hostel sweet *Khurma* or *Shakarpara* that lasts for months and that every

Indian kid living in a boarding school in the sixties or seventies would remember hoarding on.

Finally, you have the great Nizami dish, from Hyderabad, that turns ordinary bread slices in to the lip-smacking *Shahi Tukra* (Royal Slice).

In all, we discuss some twelve outstanding ways to turn the humble wheat in to great Indian desserts.

Lentils as desserts: Yuck! This may be your first reaction. After all, lentils are supposed to be bland and flavourless. How can anyone possibly think of having lentils as desserts?

Let Indian cuisine then disabuse your mind.

Just try *besan* (chick pea flour) or *moong dal* (Bengal Gram) *halwa* or the famous *motichoor laddoos*, and you would know what I'm talking about.

In addition, we discuss how to make *Boondi, Besan Laddoos* and *Imrati*.

Still don't believe us about India's robust lentil tradition? Then try out any of these six protein-filled desserts that use lentils and let us know.

Veggies as desserts: No one cooks vegetables as well and in as many ways as the Indians do. Displaying an amazing mix of tastes and aromas, Indian cuisine is perhaps the most wonderful, varied, robust, and sensual of all the cuisines in the world when it comes to vegetarianism.

But don't take our word for it. Just savour a sample of the seven great veggie puddings that we present here. We use carrots and beetroots, of course. But we also use cauliflower and bottle gourd, and even lotus seeds.

Do check out this delicious section. And we guarantee you will soon be asking for more.

Paneer or Indian fresh cottage cheese as desserts: We present as many as a dozen outstanding classics that will bowl you over. There are 6 kinds of *Sandesh* and one of *Kacha Gola* that are incidentally the lowest calorie sweet dishes in India or possibly in the world.

On the other end of the calorie chart, you will find the *Gulab Jamun*, which is one of the most popular street sweet dish in India.

And then you have the classic *Rasgulla* and *Rasmalai* along with the *Chhena Payash* and *Chhena Murki*.

In case, you can't access *Paneer* or the Indian fresh cottage cheese from your nearest supermarket, we also tell you how to make *Paneer* at home from scratch.

Khoya or thickened milk as dessert: This is one of the most popular category of sweets in India. We present eleven recipes here, including 4 kinds of *Barfis*, 3 kinds of *Kulfis* or the Indian ice-cream, 1 *Peda*, 2 kinds of *Rabri* and one type of *Kheer* that uses almonds.

This is also that category of Indian sweets that can let you use your favourite dark chocolates. We present the recipe for *chocolate barfi,* which is certainly a fusion dish, in that context.

Yoghurt as Dessert: We present six recipes, including 2 kinds of *Shrikhand* (hung curd), 1 *Mishti Doi* (sweet curd), 1 *Kalakand* and two kinds of the great Indian drink, *Lassi.*

In addition, we tell you how to make the Indian-style plain yoghurt (or Greek Yoghurt) at home.

The Raj Effect: Finally we present seven recipes that are inspired by the British Raj and are still served in some clubs that date from those times.

We have 3 kinds of Caramel Custard, 2 kinds of fruit pudding and one type of eggless custard pudding that at least the Indian Armed forces are very fond of serving in their messes.

It is in this background that we present as many as 70 mouth-watering dessert recipes that to recapitulate include 8 that use rice, 12 which are based around wheat, 12 with *paneer* or cottage cheese, 11 with *khoya* or thickened milk, and 7 with yoghurt.

In addition there are 7 desserts from the days of the British Raj that do involve some baking, if you were missing that!

And finally there are 6 desserts you can make from lentils and 7 from veggies. I'm sure you didn't think of that, did you?

And believe it or not, all of these are regularly made in my home even today.

So forget your boring boiled and baked ways to make your desserts and let this new book open your eyes to the wonderful possibilities of making sweet meats the way northern, southern, eastern and western Indians do.

And the bottom line is that you master these and you can handle any Indian sweet dish from any part of India, I promise.

Note: Please remember that the "Home Style" recipes I have catalogued here are made regularly in my home. You are strongly encouraged to experiment, adapt and add your own variation so that the dishes tastes like your "Home food."

The idea of experimentation and adaption is specifically relevant for the diabetics and the lactose-intolerant who will have to use sugar or milk-substitutes, as the case be, in the proportion or quantities as they deem fit.

A final word of warning though. If you are a complete newbie i.e. someone who does not even know how to boil an egg, I suggest you start from my first book "How To Cook In A Jiffy Even If You Have Never

Boiled An Egg Before" (**see the description towards the end of this book**).

Indian cooking can be a little tricky and it is best to acquire some basic cooking skills before making this a part of your daily routine.

Chapter 3: Rice as Desserts

"Absolutely eat dessert first. The thing that you want to do the most, do that."

–Joss Whedon

The love affair that Indians have with rice is legendary.

Rice has been a sacred grain, with some of the ancient Indian holy books like the Vedas simply referring to it as *annam*, meaning food.

Every religious ceremony has had to involve rice. Rice is stuck on the red vermillion that is applied to your forehead as *akshat*, literally meaning something which is indestructible.

Rice is poured into the holy fire lit during religious ceremonies as an offering to the gods.

Rice is sprinkled over guests, worshippers and the newlyweds to bless them.

In certain parts of India, the bride and bridegroom are made to even stand on a pile of rice during the marriage ceremony. In North India, when a bride enters her husband's house, she is made to first knock over with her right foot a small metal jar full of rice to signify that with the spilled rice she is bringing prosperity to the house.

When priests or elders bless you, they wish that your life be full of *dhan* (wealth) and *dhanya* (rice). Did you notice the similarity between the two words?

The biggest harvest festivals in India are linked to the time when rice is harvested. *Bihu* in Assam, *Pongal* in Tamil Nadu, *Onam* in Kerala and *Makar Sakranti* in North India—are all festivals where newly harvested rice is offered to the gods amidst lots of dancing and revelry that stretches over 2-3 days. In *Pongal,* the day's celebrations include an early morning ceremony of boiling rice with milk and sugar in clay pots, which is allowed to boil over, signifying prosperity.

There are also smaller festivals linked to pre-sowing, sowing, pre-transplanting, transplanting, invoking the rain gods, protecting, and pre-harvesting.

Phew! Looks like the ancient Indians had no other obsession bigger than the quality of the rice growing in their backyards!

Rice is "popular" because it is one of the easiest foods to digest.

Being totally gluten free, it is the best food for infants when they have to be weaned.

In India, rice is vital in the ceremony of *Annaprashana*, a ritualised first feeding, which is conducted in the baby's sixth or seventh month of life. Mashed boiled rice or a sweet rice pudding called *kheer* is generally fed to the child accompanied with the chanting of sacred mantras.

For young adults and old people too, who may have wheat allergies or even celiac disease, adopting a rice diet would be what every sensible doctor would prescribe as the first step to adopting a totally gluten free diet.

For the same reason, rice is great for relieving digestive disorders like diarrhoea, dysentery, colitis and even morning sickness.

This is why 70% of the world, including USA and northern Canada, grows and consumes rice.

Cooking Rice the Indian Way

Indians cook rice with anything and everything; with lentils, veggies, meat, fish, chicken and seafood. In addition, they have plain or spiced rice as a bed for curries and ground rice for making all kinds of pancakes like *appams* and *dosas*.

Rice flour is also used for crisping savouries called *pakoras*. Most temples serve as *prasadam* (blessings) the Indian rice pudding called *kheer* or *payasam*. And then in many Himalayan states, from Ladakh to Sikkim, fermented rice is used for making the potent brew called *chhang*.

However, since we are focussing on only desserts in this book, we now present eight hand-picked recipes for cooking rice as desserts.

Please also note that the recipes listed in this chapter cannot be made in a rice cooker.

Chawal Ka Kheer (Rice Pudding)

This is a simple North Indian dessert that, as we mentioned, even the gods are very fond of. So don't be surprised to be served this dish with *Pooris* (fried unleavened bread) in Hindu temples, even outside India.

Serves 3-4

Ingredients

Full cream milk-1 litre (2 US pints liquid) (4 cups)

Rice grains-2 heaped tablespoon (washed well)

Sugar to taste - (start with 3 tablespoons)

Milk Powder-2 tablespoons

Green Cardomom-2 crushed

Saffron-few strands (optional)

Method

In a heavy bottomed wok, bring the milk to boil.

Add the rice which should have been washed well.

Keep stirring on low heat making sure that NOTHING BURNS.

As the mixture begins to thicken, add the milk powder, sugar, the cardamom and the saffron.

Stir well and keep stirring for about 5 minutes.

Switch off the heat source.

That's all. Your delicious *Chawal ka Kheer* (Rice Pudding) is ready.

You can either have it hot as some like it. Or you could let it cool down, then put it in the fridge and have it chilled.

Note: Some chefs use boiled rice for this dish, which may save time, but will NOT taste as good as the traditional recipe we share here.

Prep time: 1 minute

Cooking time: 20 minutes

Total time: 21 minutes

Natun Gud Ka Kheer (Rice Pudding with Palm Jaggery)

This is an out-of-this-world dessert from Eastern India with such subtle flavours that you will just fall in love with.

Serves 3-4

Ingredients

Full cream milk-1 litre (2 US pints liquid) (4 cups)

Rice grains-2 heaped tablespoon (washed well)

Palm Jaggery (crushed) - 3 tablespoons

Milk Powder-2 tablespoons

Method

In a heavy bottomed wok, bring the milk to boil.

Add the rice which should have been washed well.

Keep stirring on low heat making sure that NOTHING BURNS.

As the mixture begins to thicken, add the milk powder.

Stir well and keep stirring for about 5 minutes.

Switch off the heat source and now add the palm jaggery.

Stir well.

Note: Please DON'T add the palm jaggery when the milk is still on the fire as this may curdle the milk.

That's all. Your *Natun Gud Kheer* is ready.

You can either have it hot as some like it. Or let it cool down, then put it in the fridge and have it chilled.

Note: Some chefs use boiled rice for this dish, which may save time, but will NOT taste as good as the traditional recipe we share here.

Prep time: 1 minute

Cooking time: 20 minutes

Total time: 21 minutes

Phirni (Ground Rice Custard)

This used to be a favourite dessert of the Muslim rulers of India. Even now you will find it being served in traditional earthen bowls on the occasion of Muslim festivals like Eid.

Serves 3-4

Ingredients

Full cream milk-1 litre (2 US pints liquid) (4 cups)

Rice grains-2 heaped tablespoon

Sugar to taste - (start with 3 tablespoons)

Milk Powder-2 tablespoons

Green Cardomom-2 crushed

Saffron-few strands dissolved in a tablespoon warm milk

Method

Wash the rice grains well and then let it dry.

Crush the same coarsely.

In a heavy bottomed wok, bring the milk to boil. Add the milk powder.

Add the coarsely ground rice.

Keep stirring on low heat making sure that NOTHING BURNS.

As the mixture begins to thicken, add the sugar, cardamom and the saffron.

Stir well and keep stirring for about 5 minutes or till the whole mixture becomes like a thick custard.

Switch off the heat source and pour the mixture into small individual servings bowl and let it set.

That's all. Your delicious *Phirni* is ready.

Let it cool down and then put it in the fridge and have it chilled.

Prep time: 10 minutes

Cooking time: 20 minutes

Total time: 30 minutes

Sweet Rice with Mango

This is a dish from the North-East India with some inspiration from the Thais, who did rule these areas for several hundred years.

Serves 3-4

Ingredients

Rice grains-1 cup (washed)

Coconut Milk-1 cup

Water-1 cup

Palm Sugar/Sugar-4 teaspoon

Ripe Mango-1 (cut into bite size pieces)

Method using a pressure cooker

Place the rice, coconut milk, water and sugar in the cooker and put it on your heat source.

Close the lid and let the cooker come to full pressure.

Reduce the heat and let it all cook for 2 more minutes.

Switch off the heat source and let the cooker cool on its own.

Take out the rice in individual serving bowls and decorate it with ripe mangoes.

You can either have it cool or at room temperature.

Method using a thick bottomed pan

Place the rice, coconut milk, water and sugar in the pan and put it on your heat source.

After the mixture boils, reduce the heat and cover the pan with the lid.

Keep checking occasionally to see if the rice has cooked and all the water and the coconut milk has been absorbed.

Switch off the heat source and let the rice cool on its own.

Take out the rice in individual serving bowls and decorate it with ripe mangoes.

You can either have it cool or at room temperature.

Prep time: 5 minutes

Cooking time: 7 minutes with a pressure cooker; 20 minutes with a pan

Total time: 12 minutes with a pressure cooker; 25 minutes with a pan

Sweet Pongal

This is a great sweet dish from South India that has to be had for the festival of *Pongal* in Tamil Nadu. Interestingly, this is one of the few Hindu festivals that falls on the fixed day of 14 January, when the sun moves from the Tropic of Capricorn to the Tropic of Cancer heralding the arrival of spring and the beginning of the harvest season.

Serves 3-4

Ingredients

Rice grains-3/4 cup

Moong Dal (Bengal Gram)-1/4 cup

Jaggery (*Gud* which is unprocessed sugar)-1 cup

Roasted Cashew nuts-2 tablespoon (fried golden and then chopped up).

The method to fry the cashew nuts:

In a small pan, add about a tablespoon of cooking oil. Put the pan on your heat source. When the oil heats up, add the cashew nuts and stir till they turn golden. Immediately remove the cashew nuts to a plate and chop. Remember if you leave the cashew nuts in the pan, the hot oil will keep roasting the cashew nuts and burn them.

Ghee (clarified butter)-2 tablespoon

Water-3 cups

Method

Wash the rice and *dal* together and let it dry for 5 minutes on an inclined plate.

If using a pressure cooker:

In a pressure cooker, put the clarified butter and put it on your heat source.

As it warms up, add the rice and lentils.

Stir well.

Add 2 cups of water and put the lid with the weight on the cooker.

After the cooker comes to full pressure (don't worry, you will hear that typical sound), switch off the heat source but do NOT release the pressure.

Let the pressure cooker cool down by itself.

Meanwhile, in a pan, melt the jaggery with 1 cup water and let it come to a boil.

Open the cooker and add the boiled jaggery to it along with the roasted cashew nuts.

Mix well.

That's all. Your *Sweet Pongal* is ready.

If using a thick bottomed pan/vessel:

In a pan/vessel, add the clarified butter and place it on your heat source.

When the butter warms up, add the rice and lentil.

Stir well.

Add 2 cups of water.

Cover the pan/vessel with a well-fitting lid.

Reduce the heat to minimum.

In other words, if cooking on gas, turn the knob to SIM (mer). Let the *Pongal* cook for 15-20 minutes.

Switch off the heat source and let the rice remain in the vessel for another 5 minutes.

Meanwhile, in another pan, melt the jaggery with 1 cup water and let it come to a boil.

Open the vessel and add the boiled jaggery to it along with the roasted cashew nuts.

Mix well.

That's all. Your *Sweet Pongal* is ready.

Prep time: 5 minutes

Cooking time: 10 minutes with a pressure cooker; 20-25 minutes with a deep pan

Total time: 15 minutes with a pressure cooker; 25-30 minutes with a deep pan

Sakkarai Pongal (Sweet rice-lentil dessert with milk)

This is another variation of the great sweet dish from South India that has to be had for the festival of *Pongal* in Tamil Nadu.

Serves 3-4

Ingredients

Rice grains-3/4 cup

Moong Dal (Bengal Gram)-1/4 cup

Jaggery (*Gud* which is unprocessed sugar)-1 cup

Roasted Cashew nuts-2 tablespoon (fried golden and then chopped up)

The method to fry the cashew nuts:

In a small pan, add about a tablespoon of cooking oil. Put the pan on your heat source. When the oil heats up, add the cashew nuts and stir till they turn golden. Immediately remove the cashew nuts to a plate and chop. Remember if you leave the cashew nuts in the pan, the hot oil will keep roasting the cashew nuts and burn them.

Raisins- 2 tablespoon

Green Cardamom (*Chhoti Elaichi*) - 3 crushed

Saffron- 9-10 strands, dissolved in 2 tablespoons of warm milk

Ghee (clarified butter)-2 tablespoon

Water-2 cups

Milk- 4 cups

Method

Wash the rice and *dal* together and let it dry for 5 minutes on an inclined plate.

If using a pressure cooker:

In a pressure cooker, put the clarified butter and put it on your heat source.

As it warms up, add the rice and lentils.

Stir well.

Add 2 cups of water and put the lid with the weight on the cooker.

After the cooker comes to full pressure (don't worry, you will hear that typical sound), switch off the heat source but do NOT release the pressure.

Let the pressure cooker cool down by itself.

Open the cooker and add the milk.

Put the cooker on the heat source and let the milk come to a boil.

Add the jaggery and let the mixture thicken.

Keep stirring gently so that the mixture doesn't burn or boil over.

Now add the dissolved saffron and the crushed cardamom.

Stir well. The consistency should now be of a thick custard.

Switch off the heat source.

Keeping aside a few raisins and roasted cashew nuts for decorating the dish, add the remaining raisins and the roasted cashew nuts.

Mix well.

Now decorate the dish with the raisins and roasted cashew nuts that you had kept aside and serve.

That's all. Your *Sakkarai Pongal* is ready.

If using a thick bottomed pan/vessel:

In a pan/vessel, add the clarified butter and place it on your heat source.

When the butter warms up, add the rice and lentil.

Stir well.

Add 2 cups of water.

Cover the pan/vessel with a well-fitting lid.

Reduce the heat to minimum.

In other words, if cooking on gas, turn the knob to SIM (mer). Let the *Pongal* cook for 15-20 minutes.

Switch off the heat source and let the rice remain in the vessel for another 5 minutes.

Open the vessel and add the milk.

Put the vessel on the heat source and let the milk come to a boil.

Add the jaggery and let the mixture thicken.

Keep stirring gently so that the mixture doesn't burn or boil over.

Now add the dissolved saffron and the crushed cardamom.

Stir well. The consistency should now be of a thick custard.

Switch off the heat source.

Keeping aside a few raisins and roasted cashew nuts for decorating the dish, add the remaining raisins and the roasted cashew nuts.

Mix well.

Now decorate the dish with the raisins and roasted cashew nuts that you had kept aside and serve.

That's all. Your *Sakkarai Pongal* is ready.

Prep time: 7 minutes

Cooking time: 20 minutes with a pressure cooker; 30-35 minutes with a deep pan

Total time: 27 minutes with a pressure cooker; 37-42 minutes with a deep pan

Sweet Chiura/Poha Kheer (Rice Flakes Pudding)

This is a simple dessert from Bihar in Eastern India that is relished by rich and poor alike.

Serves 3-4

Ingredients

Rice Flakes-1 cup

Milk-4 cups

Sugar-8 teaspoons or to taste

Method

Wash the rice flakes and drain all the water.

Light the heat source and in a wok or deep pan, bring the milk to boil.

To the boiling milk, add the sugar and let it dissolve well.

Now add the rice flakes and again let the mixture come to a boil.

Switch off the heat source.

That's all. Your Bihari *Chiura Kheer* is ready.

This dish tastes excellent hot especially with sliced ripe bananas sprinkled on it.

Prep time: 3 minutes

Cooking time: 7 minutes

Total time: 10 minutes

Murhi Chikki (Puffed Rice Praline)

Again from Bihar in Eastern India this is a sweet snack with great staying power. Even without refrigeration, it can last from 7-10 days if stored well in a dry container.

Serves 3-4

Ingredients

Puffed rice: 2 cups

Sugar: 1 cup

Ghee (clarified butter) or unsalted butter or cooking oil: 1 teaspoon for greasing the plate

Method

In a thick bottomed wok/pan, add the sugar and put it on your heat source.

As the sugar melts, gently keep stirring.

When the sugar acquires a golden brown colour evenly, switch off the heat source and add the puffed rice.

Mix well.

Pour this mixture on to a flat plate lightly greased with *ghee* (clarified butter) or cooking oil.

Let the mixture cool. You can now cut small pieces (in whatever shape you desire) and enjoy.

That's all. Your *Murhi Chikki* is ready.

If you wish to store this dish, you can do that in a zip lock or airtight container, without putting in a refrigerator.

Preparation time: 2 minutes

Cooking time: 8 minutes

Total: 10 minutes

Chapter 4: Wheat as Desserts

"Once in a young lifetime one should be allowed to have as much sweetness as one can possibly want and hold."

–Judith Olney

Wheat as a crop is not as indigenous to India as rice is. The cultivation of "emmer wheat" is supposed to have originated in the Levant region of West Asia around 9000 BCE. From there it reached Greece, Cyprus and India by 6500 BCE, Egypt shortly after 6000 BCE, and Germany and Spain by 5000 BCE.

Ancient Indians called this hardy grain *Kanak* or *Gandham*. In Hindi, it is now called *Gehun*.

The Central Asian tribes coming to India brought all kinds of Naan breads, and the baking techniques involved in their production, to India. But somehow the use of such baked stuff remained confined to the

Muslims in India. The Hindus were happy using unleavened bread in the form of *rotis, phulkas, pooris* and later *parathas.*

Today wheat is the most widely grown cereal grain in the world. Of the 25 popular species in the world, however, only 3 species namely, Bread wheat, Macaroni wheat & Emmer wheat are commercially grown in India. Still India today is the fourth largest producer of wheat in the world after Russia, the USA and China and accounts for 8.7 percent of the world's total production of wheat.

As a cereal, wheat is much more nutritious than rice. In 100 grams, wheat provides 327 calories and is an excellent source (more than 19% of the Daily Value) of multiple essential nutrients, such as protein, dietary fibre, manganese, phosphorus and niacin. Wheat is otherwise 13% water, 71% carbohydrates, 1.5% fat and 13% protein.

Using wheat in desserts is ubiquitous in Western cuisine. Just think of any pie, cake, pastry, puff or doughnut and you will be forced to use wheat.

Indians, however, don't use wheat for making "outer coverings" only. Instead, they use wheat flour straightaway, for example, in *Aatey Ka Halwa* (Whole Wheat Flour Dessert) or *Ghola Prasad* (Whole Wheat Flour Porridge).

Then they use vermicelli for making *Kheer* or *Sevian.*

Wheat flour is also used for making pancake-type dishes, the most famous of which is the *Maalpua.*

Use *gur* or jaggery and you can have the tasty breakfast dish—*Gur Paratha.*

Fry these as spirals and you get the crispy, syrupy *Jalebis.*

Fill it with nuts and dried milk (*Khoya*) and you will have *Gujias* or *Pidukias* that are great festival dishes.

And then you have the hostel sweet *Khurma* or *Shakarpara* that lasts for months.

Finally, you have the great Nizami dish, from Hyderabad, that turns ordinary bread slices in to the lip-smacking *Shahi Tukra* (Royal Slice).

In that background, we now present as many as twelve ways to turn the humble wheat in to outstanding Indian desserts.

Aatey Ka Halwa (Whole Wheat Flour Dessert)

This is quite a JIFFY dish that can be easily rustled up within 15 minutes from scratch. In India, it is such a hit that you will find this being served even as an offering to the gods in many Hindu Temples.

We use milk in this recipe, in place of water which is more commonly used, to make it more tasty and nutritious, especially for the young persons in the family.

Serves 3-4

Ingredients

Whole Wheat Flour (*Atta*)-1 cup

Sugar-1/2 cup

Clarified butter (*Ghee*)-1/4 cup

Milk-1 cup

Saffron-few strands dissolved in milk

Green Cardomom-2 crushed

Raisins-1 tablespoon

Cashew nuts-2 tablespoon

Method

In a wok, add the clarified butter and put it on your heat source.

As soon as the clarified butter warms up, add the wheat flour (*atta*) and the cashew nuts.

Stir till both become light brown and give off a lovely aroma.

Do please ensure that you don't burn the flour!

Add the sugar, raisins and the milk along with the saffron and the cardamom to the wheat flour.

Stir well till the dessert (*halwa*) dries up.

That's all. Your whole wheat flour dessert (*atte ka halwa*) is ready.

Prep time: 5 minutes

Cooking time: 7 minutes

Total time: 12 minutes

Sevai Kheer (Sweet Vermicelli Milk Pudding)

This is a very popular dessert of the Muslims in India who have to have it during *Eid*. A drier version called *Sevaiyyan* too, like its West Asian counterpart, is quite tasty.

Serves 3-4

Ingredients

Full cream milk-1 litre (2 US pints liquid) (4 cups)

Fine Brown Wheat Vermicelli (roasted)-1 heaped tablespoon

Ghee (clarified butter)-1 teaspoon

Sugar to taste - (start with 3 tablespoons)

Milk Powder-2 tablespoons

Green Cardomom-2 crushed

Raisins-25 grams or 1oz (1 + 1/2 tablespoon) (optional)

Method

In a heavy bottomed wok, bring the milk to boil.

Keep stirring the milk on low heat making sure that it DOES NOT BURN.

As it begins to thicken, add the milk powder, sugar, and the cardamom.

Stir well and keep stirring for about 5 minutes and remove from fire.

In a pan, heat the clarified butter (*Ghee*) and add the vermicelli.

Gently toss the vermicelli for about a minute.

Note: *Ghee* is just for flavour. So you can avoid it if you are cutting down on calories.

Add the vermicelli to the wok containing the thickened milk. You may add raisins if you so desire.

Boil for a minute. Switch off the heat.

Let the dish set for about 10 minutes.

That's all. Your *Sevian Kheer* is ready.

You can either have it hot as some like it. Or let it cool down and then put it in the fridge and have it when it is cold.

Some people like their *Sevian* thick and others thin. Choose the way you like it. If you like it thin, you can even avoid putting in the milk powder in the recipe given above.

Prep time: 2 minutes

Cooking time: 20 minutes

Total time: 22 minutes

Shahi Seviyan (Royal Vermicelli)

This is the drier version we were talking of in the earlier recipe of *Sevian Kheer*. Again many Muslims in India have to have it during *Eid*. The West Asian versions avoid using milk or water so as to increase the shelf-life of this dish.

Serves 3-4

Ingredients

Full cream milk-1 litre (2 US pints liquid) (4 cups)

Fine Brown Wheat Vermicelli (roasted)-100 grams (1 cup)

Ghee (clarified butter)-2 tablespoon

Sugar to taste – ½ cup

Water- ½ cup

Milk Powder-2 tablespoons

Green Cardomom-2 crushed or *Kewra* water- 2 tablespoon or Rose water- 2 tablespoon

Raisins-25 grams or 1oz (1 + 1/2 tablespoon) (optional) for garnish

Method

Make Khoya or reduce the milk

In a heavy bottomed wok, bring the milk to boil.

Keep stirring the milk on low heat making sure that it DOES NOT BURN.

As it begins to thicken, add the milk powder.

Stir well till the milk is reduced by 3/4th and becomes thick.

Remove from fire and keep aside.

Now make your sugar syrup

Place a deep pan on your heat source and add the sugar and water.

Bring to a boil.

Reduce heat and let the mixture boil for five minutes more.

Add cardamom/*kewra*/ rose water.

Keep aside.

Prepare the vermicelli

In a pan, heat the clarified butter (*Ghee*) and add the vermicelli.

Gently toss the vermicelli till it acquires a light brown colour.

Now assemble the dish

Add the fried vermicelli to the pan containing the sugar syrup.

Boil for a minute. Switch off the heat.

Now add the *khoya*/ reduced milk.

You may garnish with raisins if you so desire.

That's all. Your *Shahi Seviyan* is ready.

You can either have it hot as some like it. Or let it cool down and then put it in the fridge and have it when it is cold.

Prep time: 5 minutes

Cooking time: 25 minutes

Total time: 30 minutes

Ghola Prasad or Aatey Ka Kheer (Whole Wheat Flour Porridge)

This is not really porridge but the closest Western dish that it comes to would be porridge. This dish is usually served in Eastern India especially during some religious festivals where it is better known as *Ghola Prasad* (literally dissolved blessings).

It is also a complete meal in itself and is really filling if you choose to have it for breakfast. The browned whole wheat flour in milk imparts a really nice aroma which is very appetising. A perfect alternative to a traditional porridge, I must say.

You may try this variation if you are getting bored with your pre-packaged cereals for breakfast.

Otherwise treat this as an Indian dessert that can be prepared in around 10 minutes, and ENJOY.

Serves 3-4

Ingredients

Whole wheat flour-1 cup

Sugar-1/2 cup

Clarified butter (*Ghee*)-1 tablespoon

Milk-3 cups

Green Cardomom-2 crushed

Cashew nuts-50 grams (2oz) (3 tablespoon)

Raisins-25 grams (1oz) (1 + 1/2 tablespoon)

Almonds-25 grams (1oz) (1 + 1/2 tablespoon)

Walnuts-25 grams (1oz) (1 + 1/2 tablespoon)

Dried figs-25 grams (1oz) (1 + 1/2 tablespoon)

Dried Dates-25 grams (1oz) (1 + 1/2 tablespoon)

Method

In a wok, add the clarified butter and put it on your heat source.

As soon as the clarified butter warms up, add the wheat flour and stir till it becomes light brown and gives off a lovely aroma.

Do please ensure that you don't burn the flour!

Switch off the heat source.

Remove the wok and pour the browned flour in a bowl.

Pour in sugar, milk, cardamom and all the nuts/dry fruits.

Mix well and let the mixture cool for at least half an hour before serving.

That's all. Your *Ghola Prasad or Aatey Ki Kheer* is ready.

Prep time: 5 minutes

Cooking time: 5 minutes

Total time: 10 minutes

Suji Halwa (Semolina Dessert)

Another JIFFY dish that also tastes divine. No wonder, this is offered as *prasad* (blessing) in many Sikh *Gurudwaras*.

We use milk in this recipe, in place of water which is more commonly used, to make it more tasty and nutritious, especially for the young persons in the family.

Serves 3-4

Ingredients

Semolina (*Suji*)-1 cup

Sugar-1/2 cup

Clarified butter (*Ghee*)-1/4 cup

Milk-1 cup

Saffron-few strands dissolved in milk

Green Cardomom-2 crushed

Method

In a wok, add the clarified butter and put it on your heat source.

As soon as the clarified butter warms up, add the semolina (*suji*) and stir till it becomes light brown and gives off a lovely aroma.

Do please ensure that you don't burn the semolina!

Add the sugar and the milk along with the saffron and the cardamom to the semolina.

Stir well till the dessert (*halwa*) dries up.

That's all.

Your *Suji ka Halwa* is ready.

Prep time: 5 minutes

Cooking time: 7 minutes

Total time: 12 minutes

Shahi Tukra (The Royal Piece) or Double ka Meetha

Want to turn an ordinary bread slice in to a piece of dessert that is fit for the Royalty? Then try this lip-smacking recipe *Shahi Tukra* (literally the Royal Slice) from Hyderabad, South India.

Discovered by the innovative cooks of the Nizams, this dish is also called *Double ka Meetha*, as it is made from the common bread which the locals call "double-*roti*."

Serves 3-4

Ingredients

Bread: 6 slices

Full cream milk: 1 litre (4 cups)

Milk powder: 2 tablespoon

Sugar: 1 cup

Water: ½ cup

Ghee (clarified butter): ½ cup

Saffron: 10-12 strands dissolved in 2 tablespoon hot milk

Unsalted pistachio nuts: 3 tablespoon (approx. 50 grams)

Method

Make your Rabri/thickened milk

Place a thick-bottomed wok/pan on your heat source.

Pour in the milk and add the milk powder.

When the mixture comes to a boil, reduce the heat and keep stirring till the milk is reduced by about 75% (3/4th).

Keep aside.

While the milk thickens, toast the bread slices in a toaster till golden.

Keep aside.

Tip: Some recipes DON'T advise toasting and ask you to go straight to frying the bread slices. If you did this, you will only allow the bread to soak up too much of ghee. So if you want to economise on the use of ghee, you may like to prefer following our recipe.

Now make your sugar syrup

Place a deep pan on your heat source and add the sugar and water.

Bring to a boil.

Reduce heat and let the mixture boil for five minutes more.

Keep aside.

Tip: Some recipes ask you to boil the syrup till you get the 1-strand consistency i.e. when a drop of syrup between your fingers becomes so thick as to become a thin strand. In my opinion, this will only make the syrup cloyingly sweet, that most people in the world hate. So go by your palate!

Now take a fry pan and add the *ghee*.

Put the pan on your heat source.

As soon as the *ghee* melts, fry the toasted bread slices one by one till they are all nice and crisp.

Cut each fried slice in to four rectangular pieces and dip in the sugar syrup.

With a slotted spoon, remove the slices from the sugar syrup and place these on a serving dish.

Please don't leave these slices in the sugar syrup for long as they will then become soggy.

Use the left-over syrup to sweeten the *rabri* (thickened milk) to your taste.

Now pour this sweet *rabri*/ thickened milk over each slice.

Sprinkle the saffron and decorate with the pistachio.

That's all. Your fit-for-royalty *Shahi Tukra* or *Double ka Meetha* is ready.

Preparation time: 5 minutes

Cooking time: 30 minutes

Total time: 35 minutes.

Maal Pua

This is a great festival dish that has to be compulsorily served on the occasion of Holi, the festival of colours, especially in the Eastern Indian States of Bihar and Uttar Pradesh.

Maal Pua is now so popular that a thinner version of this dessert features on the menu of most five-star hotels in India.

Personally we don't like this latter interpretation. We present here, therefore, the original festive dish in all its glory.

Serves 3-4

Ingredients

White flour (*Maida*)-1 cup

Sugar-1 cup

Water- 1 cup

Clarified butter (*Ghee*) - enough to deep fry (quantity depend on the size of your frying pan)

Full cream Milk- 1 litre (4 cups) for making *khoya* Or *Khoya*- 250 grams (1 cup)

Full cream Milk- 750 ml (3 cups) for making the batter

Milk Powder- 2 tablespoon

Desiccated coconut- ½ cup (125 grams)

Green Cardomom-2 crushed

Cashew nuts (chopped) -50 grams (2oz) (3 tablespoon)

Raisins-25 grams (1oz) (1 + 1/2 tablespoon)

Almonds (chopped) -25 grams (1oz) (1 + 1/2 tablespoon)

Walnuts (chopped) 25 grams (1oz) (1 + 1/2 tablespoon)

Method

Make Khoya or reduce the milk

In a heavy bottomed wok, bring 1 litre (4 cups) milk to boil.

Keep stirring the milk on low heat making sure that it DOES NOT BURN.

As it begins to thicken, add the milk powder.

Stir well till the milk is reduced by 3/4th and becomes thick.

Remove from fire and keep aside.

(Note: You can avoid this step if you have access to readymade *khoya* of good quality.)

Now make the Maal Pua Batter

In a deep bowl, mix together the flour, *khoya*, and 3 cups milk.

Now add the desiccated coconut and all the dry fruits and nuts.

Mix well.

Let it set for at least 30 minutes.

Now make your sugar syrup

Place a deep pan on your heat source and add the sugar and water.

Bring to a boil.

Reduce heat and let the mixture boil for five minutes more.

Add cardamom.

Keep aside.

Fry the puas

In a fry pan (preferably non-stick), add the clarified butter and put it on your heat source.

As soon as the clarified butter heats up, add a tablespoon of the *pua* batter.

If there be space, you can add a tablespoon more of the *pua* batter.

Please ensure that the *puas* don't stick to each other.

Reduce the heat and gently flip the *puas* over with a slotted spoon to ensure that they acquire a golden-brown colour on both sides.

Do please ensure that you don't burn the *puas*!

As soon as the *puas* are fried, put them in the pan with the sugar syrup for a minute or two, and take them out on to a serving dish.

Repeat till all the batter is used up.

That's all. Your *Maal Puas* are ready.

Serve hot.

Prep time: 10 minutes (excluding 30 minutes for the batter to set)

Cooking time: 40 minutes

Total time: 50 minutes

Pua-Dry

This is the drier version of *Maal Pua*, which is preferred by some as it lasts longer. Also, this recipe can use sugar-substitutes, and so can be served to diabetics in moderation.

Serves 3-4

Ingredients

White flour (*Maida*)-1 cup

Castor Sugar-1/2 cup

Clarified butter (*Ghee*) - enough to deep fry (quantity depends on the size of your frying pan)

Full cream Milk- 750 ml (3 cups) for making the batter

Milk Powder- 2 tablespoon

Desiccated coconut- ½ cup (125 grams)

Green Cardomom-2 crushed

Cashew nuts (chopped) -50 grams (2oz) (3 tablespoon)

Raisins-25 grams (1oz) (1 + 1/2 tablespoon)

Almonds (chopped) -25 grams (1oz) (1 + 1/2 tablespoon)

Walnuts (chopped) 25 grams (1oz) (1 + 1/2 tablespoon)

Method

Make the Maal Pua Batter

In a deep bowl, mix together the flour, milk powder, sugar, cardamom, and 3 cups of milk.

Now add the desiccated coconut and all the dry fruits and nuts.

Mix well.

Let it set for at least 30 minutes.

Now fry the puas

In a fry pan (preferably non-stick), add the clarified butter and put it on your heat source.

As soon as the clarified butter heats up, add a tablespoon of the *pua* batter.

If there be space, you can add a tablespoon more of the *pua* batter.

Please ensure that the *puas* don't stick to each other.

Reduce the heat and gently flip the *puas* over with a slotted spoon to ensure that they acquire a golden-brown colour on both sides.

Do please ensure that you don't burn the puas!

As soon as the *puas* are fried, take them out on to a serving dish.

Repeat till all the batter is used up.

Serve hot or cold, as you prefer.

These dry *puas* can be taken on tours/picnics because they can last up to a week without refrigeration.

Prep time: 10 minutes (excluding 30 minutes for the batter to set)

Cooking time: 25 minutes

Total time: 35 minutes

Jalebi (Sweet Crispy Spirals)

This orange-red sugary-syrupy sweet dish is a favourite of street food vendors. It is deep fried and admittedly calorie dense. But have one and I guarantee you will not be able to resist the temptation to try one more.

Watching it being made in front of your eyes is as intriguing as the spiral shape it comes in. Watch out for the cheaper versions, however, that use artificial orange-red colours in place of the more expensive saffron that we recommend using in our "home style" recipe.

Serves 3-4

Ingredients

White flour (*Maida*)-1 cup

Rice Flour- ¼ cup

Dry Yeast- ¼ teaspoon

Yoghurt- 1 tablespoon

Saffron- 10-20 strands dissolved in warm water

Luke warm water- ½ cup

Clarified butter (*Ghee*) - enough to deep fry (quantity depends on the size of your frying pan)

For the syrup

Sugar-1 cup

Water- 1 cup

Green Cardomom-2 crushed

Method

Make the Jalebi Batter

In a deep bowl, mix together the wheat flour, rice flour, dry yeast, yoghurt, dissolved saffron, and 1/2 cup lukewarm water.

Mix well.

Let it set for at least 1 hour.

Now make your sugar syrup

Place a deep pan on your heat source and add the sugar and water.

Bring to a boil.

Reduce heat and let the mixture boil for five minutes more.

Add cardamom.

Keep aside.

Fry the jalebis

In a fry pan (preferably non-stick), add the clarified butter and put it on your heat source.

Put the jalebi batter in an icing bag with a small opening.

As soon as the clarified butter heats up, squeeze out a tablespoon of the *jalebi* batter in the shape of a circle or figure of eight.

If there be space, you can add a tablespoon more of the *jalebi* batter.

Reduce the heat and gently flip the *jalebis* over with a slotted spoon to ensure that they acquire a golden-brown colour on both sides.

Do please ensure that you don't burn the *jalebis*!

As soon as the *jalebis* are fried, take them out and put them in to the pan with the sugar syrup for a minute or two.

Take out the *jalebis* from the sugar syrup on to a serving dish.

Repeat till all the batter is used up.

That's all. Your *Jalebis are* ready.

Serve hot. With *Rabri* if you don't mind the additional calories!

Prep time: 5 minutes (excluding 60 minutes for the batter to set)

Cooking time: 25 minutes

Total time: 30 minutes

Gur Paratha (Jaggery-stuffed Fried Bread)

This is a great breakfast dish from the Eastern Indian state of Bihar.

Try this once and you will marvel at the ingenuity of Indians to come up with a dish which tastes quite like your usual pancakes served with Maple Syrup!

Serves 3-4

Ingredients

For the Paratha

Whole Wheat Flour-3 cups (enough for 5 *parathas*)

Salt-1/2 teaspoon

Cooking Oil-1 tablespoonful

Luke Warm Water-1 cup

Cooking Oil or Clarified Butter (*Ghee*) for roasting the *Parathas*; *Ghee* is preferred if you want the authentic taste.

For the filling

Gur (Jaggery)-1/2 cup

Fennel seeds (*Saunf*) -1/2 teaspoon crushed

Method

In a mixing bowl, mix together the wheat flour, salt and one tablespoon cooking oil.

Now make a firm dough by adding the water and kneading well.

Cover the dough and leave for ½ an hour.

Meanwhile crush the jaggery coarsely and mix with the crushed fennel seeds.

Now, go back to the dough and take large walnut sized balls out of it.

Flatten this ball into a patty.

In the centre of this patty, place a tablespoon of the jaggery mixture.

Close the patty from all sides so that the mixture goes in the middle and is covered well with the dough on all sides.

Again, flatten the dough gently with your hands giving it a round shape.

Cover this mixture gently with dry flour.

Place the dough on a rolling board and flatten with a rolling pin till it gets a nice round shape.

Please press evenly while rolling out so that the jaggery mixture remains covered with dough.

Now put a griddle on your heat source.

As soon as the griddle becomes hot, place the *Paratha* on it.

Reduce the heat/flame to medium and let the *Paratha* cook on one side.

Flip over and let it cook on the other side.

Take a teaspoon of oil/*Ghee* and cover the side facing you with that.

Flip over and repeat the process till the *Paratha* gets a nice, crisp texture.

Line a casserole with a paper napkin and place the *Paratha* inside it to keep it hot.

Repeat the process till all the *Parathas* are made.

That's all. Your delicious *Gur Parathas* are ready.

Prep time: 35 minutes

Cooking time: 5 minutes for 5 *parathas* @1 minute per *parathas*

Total time: 40 minutes

Gujia or Pidukia

This is a casserole kind of delicacy where a shell made of wheat flour is filled with *khoya* and nuts. In North India, this is usually served on the occasion of Holi, the spring festival of colours.

Serves 3-4

Ingredients

White Flour (*Maida*)-1 cup

Clarified butter (*Ghee*)-1/4 cup (part of dough, to add crispness to the dish)

Lukewarm Water-1/4 cup

Clarified butter (*Ghee*) - enough to deep fry (quantity depends on the size of your wok/frying pan)

For the syrup

Sugar-1 cup

Water- 1 cup

Green Cardomom-2 crushed

For the filling

Full cream milk: 1 litre (4 cups) OR *Khoya*- 250 grams (1 cup)

Milk powder: 2 tablespoon

Desiccated coconut- 2 tablespoon

Raisins- 2 tablespoon

Sugar- 3 tablespoon

Method

Making the dough for the outer cover

In a deep bowl, mix together the white flour, and the clarified butter.

Now make a firm dough by adding the lukewarm water and kneading well.

Cover the dough and leave for ½ an hour.

Now make the filling

Place a thick-bottomed wok/pan on your heat source.

Pour in the milk and add the milk powder.

When the mixture comes to a boil, reduce the heat and keep stirring till the milk is reduced and becomes almost dry.

(Note: You can avoid this step if you have access to readymade *khoya* of good quality.)

Add the desiccated coconut, 3 tablespoon sugar and raisins.

Mix well till the sugar is melted.

Keep aside.

Now make your sugar syrup

Place a deep pan on your heat source and add the 1 cup of sugar and water.

Bring to a boil.

Reduce heat and let the mixture boil for five minutes more.

Add cardamom.

Keep aside.

Tip: Some recipes ask you to boil the syrup till you get the 1-strand consistency i.e. when a drop of syrup between your fingers becomes so thick as to become a thin strand. In my opinion, this will only make the syrup cloyingly sweet, that most people in the world hate. So go by your palate!

Now assemble the dish

Go back to the dough and take large walnut sized balls out of it.

Flatten each ball into a patty.

Take a rolling pin and a rolling board and grease both lightly with some *ghee.*

Place the patty on the rolling board and flatten with a rolling pin till it acquires a round shape.

Take this into your hand and fold by half.

Place a tablespoon of the filling in between.

Take a little water in your fingers and seal the top.

Gently pinch and fold the sealed edge in to a pleated design so that the stuffing remains firmly enclosed.

Repeat till all the dough is used up.

Keep aside.

Fry the Gujias/ Pidukias

In a wok (deep sauce pan), add the clarified butter and put it on your heat source.

As soon as the clarified butter heats up, add 2-3 filled *Gujias/Pidukias* at a time.

Gently flip the *Gujias/Pidukias* over with a slotted spoon to ensure that they acquire a golden-brown colour on both sides.

Now take out the fried *Gujias/Pidukias* and put them in to the hot sugar syrup for two minutes and remove to a serving dish.

Repeat till all the *Gujias/Pidukias* are thus made.

If using an Air Fryer

Pre-heat the Air Fryer at 200 degree C (392 degrees F) for 5 minutes.

Follow all the preparatory steps listed above except making the sugar syrup till you come to deep frying in oil.

Now, with a silicon brush, gently brush the *Gujias/ Pidukias* with a little *ghee* on all sides.

Place the *Gujias/ Pidukias* in the Air Fryer in a way that all pieces remain separate and NOT on top of one another.

Air-fry for 12 minutes at 200 degree C (392 degrees F).

Repeat till all the *Gujias/ Pidukias* are air-fried.

That's all. Your *Gujias/Pidukias are* ready.

Prep time: 30 minutes

Cooking time: 20 minutes if frying in a wok; 60 minutes if using an Air Fryer

Total time: 50 minutes in a wok; 90 minutes in an Air Fryer

Khurma or Shakarpara

This is that great hostel sweet that lasts for months and that every Indian kid living in a boarding school in the sixties or seventies would remember hoarding on.

Even now, when you have access to cookies, chocolates, and of course, refrigeration, you can give this dish a try for picnics and long tours.

That is any time when you need to indulge your sweet tooth with something pure and home-made.

Serves 3-4

Ingredients

White Flour (*Maida*)-1 cup

Clarified butter (*Ghee*)-1/4 cup (part of dough, to add crispness to the dish)

Lukewarm Water-1/4 cup

Clarified butter (*Ghee*) - enough to deep fry (quantity depends on the size of your wok/frying pan)

For the syrup

Sugar-1 cup

Water- ¼ cup

Green Cardomom-2 crushed

Method

In a deep bowl, mix together the white flour, and the clarified butter.

Now make a firm dough by adding the lukewarm water.

Cover the dough and leave for ½ an hour.

Now, go back to the dough and take large walnut sized balls out of it.

Flatten this ball into a patty.

Cover this patty gently with dry flour.

Place the patty on a rolling board and flatten with a rolling pin.

The patty need not be very thin like a conventional *roti/chapatti.*

Using a knife, cut out thick, finger sized strips.

Repeat till all the dough is thus cut.

Keep aside.

Fry the Khurma

In a wok (deep sauce pan), add the clarified butter and put it on your heat source.

As soon as the clarified butter heats up, add a few cut strips of the *khurma* dough.

Gently flip the *khurmas* over with a slotted spoon to ensure that they acquire a golden-brown colour on both sides.

Repeat till all the dough is used up.

Keep aside on a serving dish.

If using an Air Fryer

Pre-heat the Air Fryer at 200 degree C (392 degrees F) for 5 minutes.

Follow all the preparatory steps listed above till you come to deep frying in oil.

Now, with a silicon brush, gently brush a few cut strips of the *khurma* dough with a little *ghee* on all sides.

Place the cut strips of the *khurma* dough in the Air Fryer in a way that all pieces remain separate and NOT on top of one another.

Air-fry for 8 minutes at 200 degree C (392 degrees F).

Repeat till all the *Khurmas* are air-fried.

Now make your sugar syrup

Place a deep pan on your heat source and add the sugar and water.

Bring to a boil.

Reduce heat and let the mixture boil for five minutes more.

Add cardamom.

Now add the fried *khurmas* to this hot sugar syrup and mix well.

That's all. Your *Khurmas are* ready.

Prep time: 10 minutes (excluding 30 minutes for the dough to set)

Cooking time: 20 minutes if frying in a wok; 60 minutes if using an Air Fryer

Total time: 30 minutes in a wok; 90 minutes in an Air Fryer

Chapter 5: Lentils as Desserts

"I'm not a vegetarian! I'm a dessertarian!"

– Bill Watterson

In ancient times lentils were considered so important that the Romans used to name their emperors after the most common legumes: Lentulus (lentil), Fabius (fava), Piso (pea), and Cicero (chickpea).

A lentil diet was considered necessary in ancient Rome to achieve a modest temper (as Pliny wrote). Ancient Romans associated lentils with prudent virtues.

Today lentils are regarded as the "Healthiest Food in the World."

This is because:

* Lentils are rich in fibre;

* Lentils are good for a healthy heart;

* Lentils replenish iron needed for energy; and

* Lentils are low in cholesterol.

No wonder, lentils are mentioned in religious books such as the Bible, Quran and the Vedas.

In a Biblical tale, lentils were a godsend to the famished Esau.

The Quran mentions that legumes were vital to the diet of the Christian community in Egypt.

Lentils are consumed during Lent, a time of fasting before Easter, in many Catholic countries. Probably the name lent comes from the Latin word "lens" meaning lentils.

Vedas tell us that men domesticated cattle and grew barley, rice and lentils.

Lentils have been uncovered in tombs and in the underground stores of the pyramids in Egypt. Egypt was known to be the leading seller of lentils in the ancient world.

It is said that without carrying *Sattu* or roasted chickpea flour with them, for sustenance on those long and arduous treks, Buddhist monks from India could NOT have spread Buddhism to far-off places from Afghanistan and Tibet to Korea!

Indians appear to have adapted and innovated recipes over hundreds or perhaps thousands of years that include lentils as the MAIN ingredient. The diversity of Lentil recipes in India is simply breathtaking and even mind-boggling at times.

Indians cook lentils with everything: rice, veggies, wheat and meats. They also have lentils as soups, snacks, main dish, and hold your breath, as DESSERTS.

Don't believe it. Then let me introduce you to six outstanding lentil desserts that can be made at home and in a JIFFY.

Besan Halwa (Chickpea Flour Dessert)

This is again one of those desserts that is considered fit for the Gods, and so is offered quite frequently in temples and at homes during religious functions.

We use milk in this recipe, in place of water which is more commonly used, to make it more tasty and nutritious, especially for the young persons in the family.

Serves 3-4

Ingredients

Chickpea flour (*Besan*)-1 cup

Sugar-1/2 cup

Clarified butter (*Ghee*)-1/4 cup

Milk-1 cup

Saffron-few strands (about 10) dissolved in milk

Green Cardomom-2 crushed

Cashew nuts-25 grams (1 oz.) (1 + 1/2 tablespoon)

Raisins-25 grams (1 oz.) (1 + 1/2 tablespoon)

Method

In a wok, add the clarified butter and put it on your heat source.

As soon as the clarified butter warms up, add the *besan* (Chickpea flour) and cashew nuts and stir till all become light brown and give off a lovely aroma.

Do please ensure that you don't burn the flour!

Add the sugar, milk along with the saffron, the cardamom and raisins to the flour.

Stir well till the dessert (*halwa*) dries up.

That's all.

Your *Besan Halwa* is ready.

Prep time: 5 minutes

Cooking time: 7 minutes

Total time: 12 minutes

Boondi

This is a dish that can be served as round *laddoos,* or mixed with yoghurt and taken as a tasty *raita.*

Or, just pop it as it is and you will be soon asking for more.

Serves 3-4

Ingredients

Chick pea flour- 1 cup

Rice flour- 2 table spoons

Green Cardamom – 5

Baking powder- ½ teaspoon

Saffron strands: few (about 10) dissolved in water

Sugar- 1 cup

Water- 1½ cup; ½ cup for making chick pea flour batter and 1 cup for making the sugar syrup

Clarified butter (*Ghee*) - enough to deep fry (quantity depends on the size of your frying pan)

Method

In a bowl, whisk together the chick pea flour, rice flour, baking powder and ½ cup water, till it gets a pouring consistency.

In case the batter becomes too dry, you may add a little more water.

Let the batter stand for a while.

Meanwhile make the sugar syrup.

In a vessel, add the sugar, water, cardamom pods (whole) and the dissolved saffron.

Put this vessel on your heat source and bring the sugar mixture to a boil.

Reduce the heat and let the mixture boil for another 5 minutes before switching off the heat source.

In a small wok, add the *ghee* and put it on your heat source.

When the *ghee* heats up, take a slotted spoon and gently pour the chickpea batter through this while shaking the slotted spoon over the ghee. This is to ensure that the batter falls into the hot *ghee* in small droplets.

Fry the droplets in batches.

As soon as one batch becomes golden brown, take it out of the *ghee* and transfer to the vessel containing the sugar syrup. Remove after 2 minutes.

Repeat till the entire batter is used up.

That's all. Your sweet *Boondi* is ready.

Have this hot or at room temperature.

Prep time: 15 minutes

Cooking time: 20 minutes

Total time: 35 minutes

Motichoor Laddoo

If you master the earlier recipe of *Boondi,* you can easily graduate to making *Motichoor Laddoos* which is a great street dessert. Just follow the directions below.

On the streets, however, do watch out for the cheaper versions that use artificial orange-red colours in place of the more expensive saffron that we prefer using in our "home style" recipe.

Serves 3-4

Ingredients

Chick pea flour- 1 cup

Green Cardamom – 5

Baking powder- ½ teaspoon

Saffron strands: few (about 10) dissolved in water

Sugar- 1 cup

Water- 1½ cup; ½ cup for making chick pea flour batter and 1 cup for making the sugar syrup

Ghee (clarified butter) - 1 cup

Method

In a bowl, whisk together the chick pea flour, baking powder and ½ cup water, till it gets a pouring consistency.

In case the batter becomes too dry, you may add a little more water.

Let the batter stand.

Meanwhile make the sugar syrup.

In a vessel, add the sugar, water, cardamom pods (whole) and the dissolved saffron.

Put this vessel on your heat source and bring the sugar mixture to a boil.

Reduce the heat and let the mixture boil for another 5 minutes before switching off the heat source.

In a small wok, add the *ghee* and put it on your heat source.

When the *ghee* heats up, take a slotted spoon and gently pour the chickpea batter through this while shaking the slotted spoon over the *ghee*. This is to ensure that the batter falls into the hot *ghee* in small droplets.

Fry the droplets in batches.

As soon as one batch becomes golden brown, take it out of the *ghee* and transfer to the vessel containing the sugar syrup. Remove after 2 minutes.

Repeat till the entire batter is used up.

Take chick pea droplets and crush it well in a blender.

Make small walnut sized balls from the crushed *boondi* with your hands and serve it on a platter.

That's all. Your delicious *Motichoor Laddoos* are ready.

Prep time: 15 minutes

Cooking time: 20 minutes

Laddoo making time: 10 minutes

Total time: 45 minutes

Moong Dal Halwa (Split Bengal Gram Dessert)

This is a simple but nutritious dessert from the Eastern Indian state of West Bengal. Easy to digest, the dish is sure to appeal to the young people in your family.

Serves 3-4

Ingredients

Split Bengal Gram *(Dhuli Moong Dal)* - ½ cup (washed and soaked in water for at least 4 hours)

Sugar-1/2 cup

Clarified butter (*Ghee*)-1/4 cup

Milk-2 cups

Saffron-few strands (about 10) dissolved in milk

Green Cardomom-2 crushed

Cashew nuts-25 grams (1 oz.) (1 + 1/2 tablespoon)

Raisins-25 grams (1 oz.) (1 + 1/2 tablespoon)

Method

In a wok, add the clarified butter and put it on your heat source.

As soon as the clarified butter warms up, add the soaked Split Bengal Gram *(Dhuli Moong Dal)* and stir till it becomes light brown and gives off a lovely aroma.

Add the sugar, milk along with the saffron, the cardamom, cashew nuts and raisins to the flour.

Stir well till the dessert (*halwa*) dries up.

That's all. Your *Moong Dal Halwa* is ready.

Prep time: 5 minutes (excluding soaking time of 4 hours)

Cooking time: 15 minutes

Total time: 20 minutes

Besan Laddoos (Chickpea Flour sweet balls)

This is again one of those desserts that has great staying power even without refrigeration.

That makes this a great dish for picnics and long tours.

And any time when you need to indulge your sweet tooth with something pure and home-made.

Serves 3-4

Ingredients

Chickpea flour (*Besan*)-1 cup

Sugar-1 cup (crushed fine)

Clarified butter (*Ghee*)-1 cup (melted)

Green Cardomom-2 crushed

Method

In a wok, add the chickpea flour (*Besan*) and put it on your heat source.

Stir well till the chickpea flour (*Besan*) becomes light brown and gives off a lovely aroma.

Do please ensure that you don't burn the flour!

Turn off the heat source and place the chickpea flour (*Besan*) in a bowl.

Add the clarified butter (*ghee*), crushed sugar and crushed green cardamom and mix well.

Make small walnut sized balls from this mixture with your hands and serve it on a platter.

That's all.

Your *Besan Laddoos* are ready.

Prep time: 5 minutes

Cooking time: 7 minutes

Total time: 12 minutes

Imarati

This is a drier and less syrupy version of that great Indian street sweet dish *Jalebi* which tastes equally divine. The addition of lentils, however, increases the nutritional quotient of *Imarati* a notch higher.

Serves 3-4

Ingredients

Split Black Gram (*Urad Dal*) -1/2 cup (soaked in water for about 4 hours)

Rice Flour- ¼ cup

Saffron- 10-20 strands dissolved in warm water

Luke warm water- ¼ cup

Baking powder- ½ teaspoon

Clarified butter (*Ghee*) - enough to deep fry (quantity depends on the size of your frying pan)

For the syrup

Sugar-1 cup

Water- 1 cup

Green Cardomom-2 crushed

Method

Make the Imarati Batter

In a grinder, grind the soaked *Urad Dal* to a fine paste, using the lukewarm water.

In a deep bowl, mix together the *Urad dal* paste, rice flour, baking powder, and the dissolved saffron.

Mix well.

The batter should be of thick, pouring consistency.

Now make your sugar syrup

Place a deep pan on your heat source and add the sugar and water.

Bring to a boil.

Reduce heat and let the mixture boil for five minutes more.

Add cardamom.

Keep aside.

Fry the *Imaratis*

In a fry pan (preferably non-stick), add the clarified butter and put it on your heat source.

Put the *Imarati* batter in an icing bag with a small opening.

As soon as the clarified butter heats up, squeeze out a tablespoon of the *Imarati* batter in the shape of a circle or figure of eight.

If there be space, you can add a tablespoon more of the *Imarati* batter.

Reduce the heat and gently flip the *Imaratis* over with a slotted spoon to ensure that they acquire a golden-brown colour on both sides.

Do please ensure that you don't burn the *Imaratis*!

As soon as the *Imaratis* are fried, take them out and put them in to the pan with the sugar syrup for a minute or two.

Take out the *Imaratis* from the sugar syrup on to a serving dish.

Repeat till all the batter is used up.

Serve hot.

That's all. Your *Imaratis* are ready.

Prep time: 10 minutes (excluding soaking time for the *Urad dal)*

Cooking time: 25 minutes

Total time: 35 minutes

Chapter 6: Making Desserts with Veggies-The Indian Way

"Life expectancy would grow by leaps and bounds if green vegetables smelled as good as bacon."

–Doug Larson

No Doug, we beg to differ. You need to come to India to see how we turn ordinary veggies into not only great curries but delicious desserts.

And, without adding any bacon, of course!

Admittedly, no one cooks vegetables as well and in as many ways as the Indians do.

For pure vegetarians India is just heaven. Vegetables are an integral part of Indian cuisine and Indians consume them in several ways. Displaying an amazing mix of tastes and aromas, Indian cuisine is perhaps the most wonderful, varied, robust, and sensual of all the cuisines in the world when it comes to vegetarianism.

But veggies as desserts?

Just savour a sample of the eight great veggie puddings that we now present.

And we guarantee you will soon be asking for more.

Gajar Ka Halwa (Carrot Halwa)

This is the classic winter dessert that you will find being served in most weddings in North India. We present, however, a short-cut and lower calorie version here.

Serves 3-4

Ingredients

Full cream milk-2 litre (4 US pints liquid) (8 cups)

Carrot-2 cup- 500 grams (grated)

Sugar to taste - (start with 6 tablespoons)

Milk Powder-6 tablespoons

Green Cardamom (*Chhoti Elaichi*)-3 crushed

Raisins- 50 grams (3 tablespoon)

Walnuts- 50 grams (chopped) (3 tablespoon)

Cashew Nuts- 50 grams (chopped) (3 tablespoon)

Ghee (clarified butter) - 2 table spoons

Method

In a heavy bottomed wok, bring the milk to boil.

Add the grated carrots.

Keep stirring on low heat making sure that NOTHING BURNS.

As the mixture begins to thicken, add the milk powder, and the cardamom.

Stir well and keep stirring till the mixture becomes almost dry.

Now add the sugar, raisins, walnuts and cashew nuts.

Keep stirring till all the sugar is melted and well blended and the mixture again becomes dry.

Now add the *ghee* and stir for five more minutes.

Switch off the heat source.

That's all. Your delicious *Gajar ka Halwa* (Carrot *Halwa*) is ready.

You can either have it hot as some like it. Or you could let it cool down and then put it in the fridge and have it when it is cold.

Note: For some strange reason, commercial preparations of this dish boil the grated carrots first in water and then mix *ghee* and *khoya* with it. That in my experience makes the dessert too greasy and NOT as tasty as the traditional recipe we share above.

Prep time: 10 minute

Cooking time: 60 minutes

Total time: 70 minutes

Gobi Ka Kheer (Cauliflower Pudding)

This is a take on that North Indian dessert *Kheer* that is otherwise so common place. So don't be surprised to be served this *Kheer* when it is cauliflower season.

Serves 3-4

Ingredients

Full cream milk-1 litre (2 US pints liquid) (4 cups)

Cauliflower-1 cup- 250 grams (washed and chopped)

Sugar to taste - (start with 3 tablespoons)

Milk Powder-2 tablespoons

Green Cardamom (*Chhoti Elaichi*)–2 crushed

Saffron-few strands (optional)

Method

In a heavy bottomed wok, bring the milk to boil.

Add the chopped cauliflower.

Keep stirring on low heat making sure that NOTHING BURNS.

As the mixture begins to thicken, add the milk powder, sugar, the cardamom and the saffron.

Stir well and keep stirring for about 5 minutes.

Switch off the heat source.

That's all. Your delicious *Gobi ka Kheer* (Cauliflower Pudding) is ready.

You can let it cool down, then put it in the fridge and have it when it is cold.

Prep time: 5 minute

Cooking time: 20 minutes

Total time: 25 minutes

Lauki Ka Kheer (Bottle Gourd Pudding)

Ever imagined turning the humble, and rather tasteless, bottle gourd into a tasty dessert? No? Then read on.

Serves 3-4

Ingredients

Full cream milk-1 litre (2 US pints liquid) (4 cups)

Bottle Gourd-2 cup- 500 grams (grated)

Sugar to taste - (start with 3 tablespoons)

Milk Powder-6 tablespoons

Green Cardamom (*Chhoti Elaichi*)–2 crushed

Method

In a heavy bottomed wok, bring the milk to boil.

Add the grated bottle gourd.

Keep stirring on low heat making sure that NOTHING BURNS.

As the mixture begins to thicken (which will take some time as the bottle gourd releases a lot of water), add the milk powder, sugar, and the cardamom.

Stir well and keep stirring for about 5 minutes.

Switch off the heat source.

That's all. Your delicious *Lauki ka Kheer* (Bottle Gourd Pudding) is ready.

You can let it cool down, then put it in the fridge and have it when it is cold.

Some people like their *Lauki ka Kheer* thick and others thin. Choose the way you like it. If you like it thin, you can even avoid putting in the milk powder in the recipe given above.

Prep time: 5 minute

Cooking time: 30 minutes

Total time: 35 minutes

Makhane Ka Kheer (Lotus Seed Pudding)

Makhana or lotus seeds, also called fox nut or gorgon nut, have been used extensively in traditional Oriental and Chinese medicine for their nutritional and healing properties. However, being low in fat and high in carbohydrates, these are nutritionally distinct from other nuts and seeds.

Lotus seeds are a good source of protein, carbohydrates, fibre, magnesium, potassium, phosphorus, iron and zinc. Their low sodium and high magnesium content makes them useful for those suffering from heart diseases, high blood pressure, diabetes and obesity.

You can eat them salted, like salted cashew nuts, or as a sweet pudding. We share the recipe for the latter here.

Serves 3-4

Ingredients

Full cream milk-1 litre (2 US pints liquid) (4 cups)

Lotus Seeds-1 cup- 250 grams

Sugar to taste - (start with 3 tablespoons)

Milk Powder-6 tablespoons

Green Cardamom (*Chhoti Elaichi*)-2 crushed

Method

Submerge the lotus seeds in a bowl of water for 2 minutes (to soften them up) and then take out and squeeze out the water.

Keep aside.

In a heavy bottomed wok, bring the milk to boil.

As the mixture begins to thicken, add the milk powder, sugar, and the cardamom.

Now add the lotus seeds.

Keep stirring on low heat making sure that NOTHING BURNS.

Stir well and keep stirring for about 5 minutes.

Switch off the heat source.

That's all. Your delicious *Makhane ka Kheer* (Lotus Seed Pudding) is ready.

You can either have it hot as some like it. Or you could let it cool down, then put it in the fridge and have it when it is cold.

Prep time: 5 minute

Cooking time: 20 minutes

Total time: 25 minutes

Gajar Ka Kheer (Carrot Pudding)

Yet another version of the classic winter dessert that you will find being served in many functions in North India.

Serves 3-4

Ingredients

Full cream milk-1 litre (2 US pints liquid) (4 cups)

Carrot-1 cup- 250 grams (grated)

Sugar to taste - (start with 3 tablespoons)

Milk Powder-4 tablespoons

Green Cardamom (*Chhoti Elaichi*)-2 crushed

Method

In a heavy bottomed wok, bring the milk to boil.

Add the grated carrots.

Keep stirring on low heat making sure that NOTHING BURNS.

As the mixture begins to thicken, add the milk powder, sugar, and the cardamom.

Stir well and keep stirring for about 5 minutes.

Switch off the heat source.

That's all. Your delicious *Gajar* ka *Kheer* (Carrot Pudding) is ready.

You can let it cool down, then put it in the fridge and have it when it is cold.

Some people like their *Gajar ka Kheer* thick and others thin. Choose the way you like it. If you like it thin, you can even avoid putting in the milk powder in the recipe given above.

Prep time: 5 minute

Cooking time: 25 minutes

Total time: 30 minutes

Lauki Ki Barfi (Bottle Gourd Sweets)

Yet another way to turn the humble, and rather tasteless, bottle gourd into a tasty sweet meat.

Serves 3-4

Ingredients

Full cream milk-1 litre (2 US pints liquid) (4 cups)

Bottle Gourd-2 cup- 500 grams (grated)

Sugar - 1 cup

Milk Powder-6 tablespoons

Green Cardamom (*Chhoti Elaichi*)-2 crushed

Melon Seeds- 2 tablespoon (optional)

Ghee (Clarified butter) - 1 tea spoon

Method

In a heavy bottomed wok, bring the milk to boil.

As the mixture begins to thicken, add the milk powder.

Keep stirring on low heat making sure that NOTHING BURNS.

When the milk is totally reduced, switch off the heat source and keep aside.

In another vessel, add the sugar and put it on your heat source.

As soon as the sugar starts to melt, add the grated bottle gourd.

Stir well and keep stirring till the mixture starts drying.

Add the green cardamom.

Switch off the heat source.

Take a plate and coat it with the *Ghee*.

Pour the bottle gourd mixture on it and flatten with a spoon.

Cover it evenly with the reduced milk.

Sprinkle over the melon seeds.

After it cools down, cut into squares.

That's all. Your delicious *Lauki ki Barfi* (Bottle Gourd Sweet) is ready.

Prep time: 5 minute

Cooking time: 60 minutes

Total time: 65 minutes

Chukandar Ka Halwa (Beetroot Halwa)

Inspired by the more popular *Gajar Halwa*, this one is a stunner visually because of its bright black-red colour.

Serves 3-4

Ingredients

Full cream milk-2 litre (4 US pints liquid) (8 cups)

Beettroot-2 cup- 500 grams (peeled and grated)

Sugar to taste - (start with 5 tablespoons)

Milk Powder-6 tablespoons

Green Cardamom (*Chhoti Elaichi*)-3 crushed

Ghee (clarified butter) - 2 table spoons

Method

In a heavy bottomed wok, bring the milk to boil.

Add the grated beetroots.

Keep stirring on low heat making sure that NOTHING BURNS.

As the mixture begins to thicken, add the milk powder, and the cardamom.

Stir well and keep stirring till the mixture becomes almost dry.

Now add the sugar and keep stirring till all the sugar is melted and well blended and the mixture again becomes dry.

Now add the *ghee* and stir for five more minutes.

Switch off the heat source.

That's all. Your delicious *Chukandar ka Halwa* (Beetroot *Halwa*) is ready.

You can either have it hot as some like it. Or you could let it cool down, then put it in the fridge and have it when it is cold.

Note: For some strange reason, commercial preparations of this dish boil the grated beet first in water and then mix *ghee* and *khoya* with it. That in my experience makes the dessert too greasy and NOT as tasty as the traditional recipe we share above.

Prep time: 10 minute

Cooking time: 60 minutes

Total time: 70 minutes

Chapter 7: Paneer as Desserts

"A dessert without cheese is like a beautiful woman with only one eye."

–Anthelme Brillat-Savarin

Indians couldn't agree more. Except that when Indians use cheese for desserts, they generally mean their own fresh cottage cheese that is called *paneer* in North India and *chhena* in East India.

How to make Paneer

For those who don't know, *Paneer* is some kind of uncured, fresh common cheese which is very popular in North Indian cuisine for savoury dishes and in East Indian cuisine for sweet meats. It is unlike any other cheese we have tasted anywhere in the world.

Many of my non-Indian friends, when asked what they like best about Indian cuisine, have quoted

Paneer recipes like *Mattar Paneer*, *Palak Paneer* or the Bengali sweet *Sandesh*.

However, if you don't live in India, you may have some difficulty finding ready-made *Paneer* in your local supermarket.

If that be so, you don't need to feel disheartened. We have a solution right here.

Here is how you can make *Paneer* easily at home and then go on to prepare your favourite sweet or savoury *Paneer* dish:

Ingredients

Whole Milk-1 litre (4 cups)

(If you wish to use toned or double-toned milk, skimmed or semi-skimmed milk, or whatever you call it, you can, but you will then get less paneer in quantity.)

Fresh squeezed lemon juice-1 tablespoon -

Method

Bring the milk to a full boil.

Add the lemon juice to the boiling milk. Stir well.

The milk will start curdling. Let it curdle fully.

Switch off the heat source.

Put a muslin cloth over a big colander, place this over a vessel and pour in it the curdled milk. The solids which remain on the muslin cloth is called *paneer*.

Let all the water drip from the *paneer*, for about an hour.

Cut the *paneer* into bite size pieces and use as you wish.

Enjoy!

Making sweets from paneer

Now that you know how to get fresh *paneer* anywhere in the world, we can discuss how to make sweets out of this wonderful material.

We present as many as a dozen outstanding classics in the following pages that will bowl you over. There are 6 kinds of *Sandesh* and one of *Kacha Gola* that are incidentally the lowest calorie sweet dishes in India or possibly the world.

On the other end of the calorie chart, you will find the *Gulab Jamun*, which is one of the most popular street sweet dish in India.

And then we present the classic *Rasgulla* and *Rasmalai* along with the *Chhena Payash* and *Chhena Murki*.

Read on.

Sandesh (Cottage Cheese Sweet)

This is the classic Eastern Indian sweetmeat that Bengalis are so fond of. Western palates may enjoy its moderate sweet taste more.

Serves 3-4

Ingredients

Fresh *Paneer* (cottage cheese)-1/2 kg (18oz) (2 cups)

Sugar-250 grams (9oz) (1 cup)

Milk Powder–3 tablespoons

Green Cardamom-3 crushed

Method

In a thick bottomed wok, mix together all the ingredients.

Place the wok on your heat source.

Keep stirring till all the water dries up and the consistency becomes thick.

Pour it all into a food processor and blend well.

Pour the mixture into a big plate or serving dish and let it cool down.

Now pick up small portions and make it into any shape with your hands or by using any moulds.

That's all. Your basic *Sandesh* is ready.

Prep time: 5 minutes

Cooking time: 10 minutes

Total time: 15 minutes

Kesari Sandesh (Cottage Cheese Sweet with Saffron)

This is when you wish to infuse the basic *Sandesh* with the aroma and colour of saffron.

Serves 3-4

Ingredients

Fresh *Paneer* (cottage cheese)-1/2 kg (18oz) (2 cups)

Sugar-250 grams (9oz) (1 cup)

Milk Powder—3 tablespoons

Saffron: about 20 strands dissolved in 2 tablespoon hot milk

Method

In a thick bottomed wok, mix together all the ingredients.

Place the wok on your heat source.

Keep stirring till all the water dries up and the consistency becomes thick.

Pour it all into a food processor and blend well.

Pour the mixture into a big plate or serving dish and let it cool down.

Now pick up small portions and make it into any shape with your hands or by using any moulds.

That's all. Your *Kesari Sandesh* is ready.

Prep time: 5 minutes

Cooking time: 10 minutes

Total time: 15 minutes

Narangi Sandesh (Cottage Cheese Sweet with Orange)

Don't have saffron? Try this orange variation then.

Serves 3-4

Ingredients

Fresh *Paneer* (cottage cheese)-1/2 kg (18oz) (2 cups)

Sugar-250 grams (9oz) (1 cup)

Milk Powder–3 tablespoons

Orange essence- 2-3 drops

Orange colour (food grade) - 2-3 drops

Candied orange peel - 1 tablespoon

Method

In a thick bottomed wok, mix together all the ingredients.

Place the wok on your heat source.

Keep stirring till all the water dries up and the consistency becomes thick.

Pour it all into a food processor and blend well.

Pour the mixture into a big plate or serving dish and let it cool down.

Now pick up small portions and make it into any shape with your hands or by using any moulds.

That's all. Your *Narangi Sandesh* is ready.

Prep time: 5 minutes

Cooking time: 10 minutes

Total time: 15 minutes

Gulab Sandesh (Rose Cottage Cheese Sweet)

This is a flavour that Persians just love.

Serves 3-4

Ingredients

Fresh *Paneer* (cottage cheese)-1/2 kg (18oz) (2 cups)

Sugar-250 grams (9oz) (1 cup)

Milk Powder–3 tablespoons

Rose water-2 tablespoon

Rose essence- 2-3 drops

Method

In a thick bottomed wok, mix together all the ingredients, except the rose water and essence.

Place the wok on your heat source.

Keep stirring till all the water dries up and the consistency becomes thick.

Pour it all into a food processor along with the rose water and the essence.

Blend well.

Pour the mixture into a big plate or serving dish and let it cool down.

Now pick up small portions and make it into any shape with your hands or by using any moulds.

That's all. Your *Gulab Sandesh* is ready.

Prep time: 5 minutes

Cooking time: 10 minutes

Total time: 15 minutes

Vanilla Sandesh (Vanilla Cottage Cheese Sweet)

Prefer the more familiar vanilla. No problems, *Sandesh* can handle that too.

Serves 3-4

Ingredients

Fresh *Paneer* (cottage cheese)-1/2 kg (18oz) (2 cups)

Sugar-250 grams (9oz) (1 cup)

Milk Powder–3 tablespoons

Vanilla essence- 2-3 drops

Method

In a thick bottomed wok, mix together all the ingredients, except the vanilla essence.

Place the wok on your heat source.

Keep stirring till all the water dries up and the consistency becomes thick.

Pour it all into a food processor.

Now add the vanilla essence.

Blend well.

Pour the mixture into a big plate or serving dish and let it cool down.

Now pick up small portions and make it into any shape with your hands or by using any moulds.

That's all. Your Vanilla *Sandesh* is ready.

Prep time: 5 minutes

Cooking time: 10 minutes

Total time: 15 minutes

Natun Gud Sandesh (Cottage Cheese Sweet with Palm Jaggery)

This is yet another legendary Eastern Indian sweetmeat that the Bengalis just love.

Serves 3-4

Ingredients

Fresh *Paneer* (cottage cheese)-1/2 kg (18oz) (2 cups)

Palm jaggery-150 grams (5oz) (half cup)

Sugar-100 grams (3.5oz) (half cup)

Milk Powder–3 tablespoons

Method

In a thick bottomed wok, mix together all the ingredients.

Place it on your heat source.

Keep stirring till all the water dries up and the consistency becomes thick.

Pour into a food processor and blend well.

Pour the mixture into a big plate or serving dish and let it cool down.

Now pick up small portions and make it into any shape with your hands or by using any moulds.

That's all. Your *Natun Gud Sandesh* is ready.

Prep time: 5 minutes

Cooking time: 10 minutes

Total time: 15 minutes

Kachha Gola (Sweet Cottage Cheese Balls)

This too is a classic Eastern Indian or rather Bengali sweetmeat.

Serves 3-4

Ingredients

Fresh *Paneer* (cottage cheese)-1/2 kg (18oz) (2 cups)

Sugar-250 grams (9oz) (half cup)

Milk Powder–3 tablespoon

Rose water-few drops

Method

In a thick bottomed wok, mix together all the ingredients EXCEPT ROSE WATER.

Place it on your heat source.

Keep stirring till all the water dries up and the consistency becomes thick.

Pour the mixture into a big plate or serving dish and let it cool down.

Add the rose water.

Now pick up small portions and make it into any shape with your hands or by using any moulds. Traditionally, it is made like small balls.

That's all. Your *Kacha Gola* is ready.

Prep time: 5 minutes

Cooking time: 10 minutes

Total time: 15 minutes

Gulaab Jamun (Black Cottage Cheese Balls)

This is the famous street sweet dish that you will find almost everywhere in India.

Serves 3-4

Ingredients

Fresh *Paneer* (cottage cheese) - 250 grams (9oz) (1 cup)

White flour (*Maida*) – 2 tablespoon

Baking powder- 1 teaspoon

Milk Powder–2 tablespoons

Green Cardamom-3 crushed

Clarified butter (*Ghee*) - enough to deep fry (quantity depend on the size of your frying pan)

For the syrup

Sugar-1 cup

Water- 1 cup

Green Cardomom-2 crushed

Method

In a vessel, mix together the *paneer*, flour, baking powder, milk powder and 3 crushed green cardamom.

Knead well till you get a greasy feeling in your hands.

Now pick up small portions and make it into small balls, of the size of marbles, with your hands. The balls swell up, when fried; so keep them small.

Keep aside.

Make your sugar syrup

Place a deep pan on your heat source and add the sugar and water.

Bring to a boil.

Add cardamom.

Keep aside.

Tip: Some recipes ask you to boil the syrup till you get the 1-strand consistency i.e. when a drop of syrup between your fingers becomes so thick as to become a thin strand. In my opinion, this will only make the syrup cloyingly sweet, that most people in the world hate. So go by your palate!

Now fry your Gulab Jamuns

In a small wok, add the *ghee* and put it on your heat source.

When the *ghee* heats up, put a few balls in and let these fry till they are brown all over. Use a slotted spoon for gently turning over the balls.

As soon as one batch becomes, take it out of the *ghee* and transfer to the vessel containing the sugar syrup.

Repeat till all the balls are fried and are placed in the sugar syrup.

Remove the wok and now place the pan with the sugar syrup and balls on your heat source.

Bring to a boil and let these boil for five minutes.

That's all. Your *Gulab Jamuns* are ready.

Prep time: 10 minutes

Cooking time: 10 minutes

Total time: 20 minutes

Chhena Payash (Cottage Cheese Pudding)

This is the simplest sweet dish that you can make from *paneer*. Quite like the *kheer* that we have discussed at so many other places.

Serves 3-4

Ingredients

Full cream milk-1 litre (2 US pints liquid) (4 cups)

Sugar to taste - (start with 4 tablespoons)

Milk Powder-2 tablespoons

Fresh *Paneer* (cottage cheese) - 250 grams (9oz) (1 cup)- cut in to 1" bite size cubes

Green Cardomom-2 crushed

Saffron- 10-12 strands (dissolved in 2 tablespoon of warmed milk)

Method

In a heavy bottomed wok/ deep sauce pan, bring the milk to a boil.

Add the *paneer* cubes.

Keep stirring on low heat making sure that NOTHING BURNS.

As the mixture begins to thicken, add the milk powder, sugar, the cardamom and the saffron.

Stir well and keep stirring for about 5 minutes.

Switch off the heat source.

That's all.

Your delicious *Chhena Payash* (Cottage Cheese Pudding) is ready.

Put it in the fridge and have it chilled.

Prep time: 5 minutes

Cooking time: 15 minutes

Total time: 20 minutes

Chhena Murki

Just another way to turn *paneer* in to a great sweet that can be taken on picnics and tours.

Serves 3-4

Ingredients

Fresh *Paneer* (cottage cheese) - 250 grams (9oz) (1 cup)- cut in to 1" bite size cubes

Sugar-1 cup (250 grams)

Water- ¼ cup

Rose Essence- 2-3 drops

Method

Place a deep pan on your heat source and add the sugar and the water.

Bring to a boil.

Add the *paneer* cubes.

Reduce heat and let the mixture boil for five minutes more.

Add rose essence.

Let the mixture boil till it is almost dry.

Remove from the heat and let it cool down.

That's all. Your *Chhena Murki* is ready.

Prep time: 5 minutes

Cooking time: 20 minutes

Total time: 25 minutes

Rasgulla (Cottage Cheese balls in sugar syrup)

This is the classic *paneer* sweet that can be found almost everywhere in the streets of West Bengal. Tinned, these are exported throughout the world by many famous Bengali, North Indian and Rajasthani sweetmeat outlets.

Serves 3-4

Ingredients

Fresh *Paneer* (cottage cheese) - 250 grams (9oz) (1 cup)

For the syrup

Sugar-1 cup

Water- 3 cups

Rose water-2 tablespoon

Rose essence- 2-3 drops

Method

In a vessel, knead well the *paneer* till you get a greasy feeling in your hands.

Now pick up small portions and make it into small balls, of the size of marbles, with your hands. The balls swell up, when cooked; so keep them small.

Keep aside.

Make your sugar syrup

Place a deep wide pan on your heat source and add the sugar and the water.

Bring to a boil.

Add all the *paneer* balls and let these boil for 20 minutes.

Don't stir the balls, as they can break.

Switch off your heat source.

Add the rose water and essence.

Let it all cool where after you can put it in the fridge.

That's all. Your *Rasgullas* are ready.

Enjoy cold.

Prep time: 10 minutes

Cooking time: 25 minutes

Total time: 35 minutes

Ras Malai (Cottage Cheese Sweet in thickened Milk)

Once you have access to *Rasgullas*, you can easily graduate to this famous North Indian dessert. Here's the recipe.

Serves 3-4

Ingredients

Rasgullas – 10 (Use tinned ones or follow the recipe above to make these yourself.)

Full cream milk: 1 litre (4 cups)

Milk powder: 2 tablespoon

Sugar: 6 teaspoons, if using fresh homemade *rasgullas*. (NIL if using tinned ones.)

Saffron: 10-12 strands dissolved in 2 tablespoon hot milk

Unsalted pistachio nuts: 3 tablespoon (approx. 50 grams)

Method

Place a thick-bottomed wok/pan on your heat source.

Pour in the milk, add the milk powder and the saffron (and sugar if using fresh *rasgullas*).

When the mixture comes to a boil, reduce the heat and keep stirring till the milk is reduced somewhat.

Now add the *rasgullas* and the pistachio and let these cook till the milk is reduced to half.

That's all. Your delicious *Rasmalai* is ready.

Preparation time: 5 minutes (excluding the time to make *rasgullas*)

Cooking time: 25 minutes

Total time: 30 minutes.

Chapter 8: *Khoya*/Thickened Milk as Dessert

"It's the finale. It's the last impression. A bad dessert can ruin the meal."

–Anne McManus

India has had the reputation of being a land of milk and honey from times immemorial. Little wonder, today it is the number 1 country in terms of milk production in the world. Lack of adequate refrigeration facilities, however, have made Indians come up with all kinds of ways to preserve milk. This includes turning milk into *paneer* and some kinds of cured cheese.

Khoya, literally meaning "lost" (water?), or thickened milk, was another way to achieve that same objective, albeit in a very tasty manner.

As a result, sweets containing *khoya* form one of the most popular category of sweets in India. We present eleven recipes in the chapter here, including 4 kinds of *Barfis*, 3 kinds of *Kulfis* or the Indian ice-cream, 1 *Peda*, 2 kinds of *Rabri* and one type of *Kheer* that uses almonds.

This is also that rare category of Indian sweets that can let you use your favourite dark chocolates. We present the recipe for *chocolate barfi,* which is certainly quite a fusion dish, in that context.

Peda Kesari (Saffron Thickened Milk Patties)

This is a sweetmeat that is generally favoured by the temple towns of Mathura or Gaya in North/ East India.

Serves 3-4

Ingredients

Full cream milk: 2 litres (8 cups)

Milk powder: 1 cup (250 grams)

Sugar- 1 cup (250 grams)

Saffron: about 20 strands dissolved in 2 tablespoon hot milk

Ghee (clarified butter) – 1 teaspoon for greasing a serving plate

Method

Place a thick-bottomed wok/pan on your heat source.

Pour in the milk and add the milk powder.

When the mixture comes to a boil, reduce the heat and keep stirring till the milk is reduced and becomes almost dry.

Add the sugar and the saffron.

Mix well till the sugar is melted and the mixture is again dry.

Switch off the heat source.

Pour this mixture on to a flat plate lightly greased with *ghee* (clarified butter).

Let the mixture cool. You can now cut small pieces (in whatever shape you desire) and enjoy.

That's all. Your *Peda Kesari* is ready.

Prep time: 5 minutes

Cooking time: 30 minutes

Total time: 35 minutes

Milk Caramel Barfi

Serves 3-4

Ingredients

Full cream milk: 2 litres (8 cups)

Milk powder: 1 cup (250 grams)

Sugar- 1 and a 1/2 cup (375 grams)

Ghee (clarified butter) – 1 teaspoon for greasing a serving plate

Method

Place a thick-bottomed wok/pan on your heat source.

Pour in the milk and add the milk powder.

When the mixture comes to a boil, reduce the heat and keep stirring till the milk is reduced and becomes almost dry.

At the same time, place another thick-bottomed wok/pan on your heat source and put the sugar for caramelising.

Gently stir till all the sugar melts and gets a golden brown colour.

Switch off this heat source.

Now pour this molten sugar in to the vessel containing the dried milk.

BE CAREFUL, BECAUSE THE MILK WILL TEND TO BOIL OVER.

Mix well till the mixture is dry again.

Switch off the heat source.

Pour this mixture on to a flat plate lightly greased with *ghee* (clarified butter).

Let the mixture cool. You can now cut small pieces (in whatever shape you desire) and enjoy.

That's all. Your *Milk Caramel Barfi* is ready.

Prep time: 5 minutes

Cooking time: 30 minutes

Total time: 35 minutes

Chocolate Barfi

This is the sweet that infuses the goodness of chocolates in to a true-blue Indian dish.

Serves 3-4

Ingredients

Full cream milk: 2 litres (8 cups)

Milk powder: 1 cup (250 grams)

Sugar- 1 cup (250 grams)

Cocoa powder: 2 tablespoon dissolved in 4 tablespoon hot milk

Ghee (clarified butter) – 1 teaspoon for greasing a serving plate

Method

Place a thick-bottomed wok/pan on your heat source.

Pour in the milk and add the milk powder.

When the mixture comes to a boil, reduce the heat and keep stirring till the milk is reduced and becomes almost dry.

Add the sugar and the dissolved cocoa powder.

Mix well till the sugar is melted and the mixture is again dry.

Switch off the heat source.

Pour this mixture on to a flat plate lightly greased with *ghee* (clarified butter).

Let the mixture cool. You can now cut small pieces (in whatever shape you desire) and enjoy.

That's all. Your *Chocolate Barfi* is ready.

Prep time: 5 minutes

Cooking time: 30 minutes

Total time: 35 minutes

Nariyal Barfi (Coconut Barfi with fresh coconut)

Yet another variation, this time infused with the goodness of fresh coconut.

Serves 3-4

Ingredients

Full cream milk: 2 litres (8 cups)

Milk powder: 1 cup (250 grams)

Sugar- 1 cup (250 grams)

Fresh coconut- 1 (grated)

Desiccated coconut- 2 tablespoon

Green cardamom- 2 crushed

Ghee (clarified butter) – 1 teaspoon for greasing a serving plate

Method

Place a thick-bottomed wok/pan on your heat source.

Pour in the milk and add the milk powder.

When the mixture comes to a boil, reduce the heat and keep stirring till the milk is reduced and becomes almost dry.

Add the sugar, green cardamom and the fresh coconut.

Mix well till the sugar is melted and the mixture is again dry.

Now add the desiccated coconut and mix well.

Switch off the heat source immediately.

Pour this mixture on to a flat plate lightly greased with *ghee* (clarified butter).

Let the mixture cool. You can now cut small pieces (in whatever shape you desire) and enjoy.

That's all. Your *Nariyal Barfi* is ready.

Prep time: 5 minutes

Cooking time: 30 minutes

Total time: 35 minutes

Nariyal Barfi in a JIFFY (Short-cut Coconut Barfi)

When you want to have home-made coconut *barfi* but don't have the time to make the classic version...........

Serves 3-4

Ingredients

Sweetened condensed milk: 1 cup (250 grams)

Desiccated coconut- 2 cups (500 grams)

Green cardamom- 2 crushed

Method

In a thick-bottomed wok/pan, mix together all the ingredients mentioned above.

Place the wok/pan now on your heat source.

Mix well till the mixture is dry.

Switch off the heat source.

Pour this mixture on to a flat plate.

Let the mixture cool. You can now cut small pieces (in whatever shape you desire) and enjoy.

That's all. Your *Nariyal Barfi in a JIFFY* is ready.

Prep time: 5 minutes

Cooking time: 10 minutes

Total time: 15 minutes

Kulfi-Mango (Indian Ice cream with Mango)

When someone said that "Ice cream is happiness condensed," Indians couldn't agree more. So here is the recipe of a classic eggless Indian ice cream paired with that sweet and juicy, quintessentially Indian summer fruit, mango.

Serves 3-4

Ingredients

Full cream milk: 2 litres (8 cups)

Milk powder: 1 cup (250 grams)

Mango puree- 1 cup (250 grams)

Sugar- 1 cup (250 grams) or to taste depending on how sweet the mango puree is.

Method

Place a thick-bottomed wok/pan on your heat source.

Pour in the milk and add the milk powder.

When the mixture comes to a boil, reduce the heat and keep stirring till the milk is reduced by half.

Add the sugar.

Mix well till the sugar is melted and the mixture gets the consistency of custard.

Switch off the heat source.

Now add the mango puree and mix well.

Let the mixture cool and then pour it in to *kulfi* or popsicle moulds.

Freeze for at least eight hours.

That's all. Your *Mango Kulfi* is ready.

Prep time: 5 minutes

Cooking time: 30 minutes

Total time: 35 minutes (excluding freezing time)

Kulfi-Badaam (Indian Ice Cream with Almonds)

Yet another Indian ice cream recipe from the time of the Mughals. Have a bite and you are sure to sing, "Me and ice cream. Best friends forever...."

Serves 3-4

Ingredients

Full cream milk: 2 litres (8 cups)

Milk powder: 1 cup (250 grams)

Sugar- 1 cup (250 grams)

Saffron- about 20 strands dissolved in 2 tablespoon hot milk

Almonds- about 20 blanched and chopped

Method

Place a thick-bottomed wok/pan on your heat source.

Pour in the milk and add the milk powder.

When the mixture comes to a boil, reduce the heat and keep stirring till the milk is reduced by half.

Add the sugar, saffron and the almonds.

Mix well till the sugar is melted and the mixture gets the consistency of custard.

Switch off the heat source.

Let the mixture cool and then pour it in to *kulfi* or popsicle moulds.

Freeze for at least eight hours.

That's all. Your *Badaam Kulfi* is ready.

Prep time: 5 minutes

Cooking time: 30 minutes

Total time: 35 minutes (excluding freezing time)

Kulfi Dry Fruits

Yet another Mughlai version of the classic Indian ice cream.

"There's nothing wrong with me a little ice cream won't fix."

–Author Unknown

Serves 3-4

Ingredients

Full cream milk: 2 litres (8 cups)

Sugar- 1 cup (250 grams)

Saffron- about 20 strands dissolved in 2 tablespoon hot milk

Almonds- 1 tablespoon blanched and chopped

Cashew nuts- 1 tablespoon

Poppy seeds- 1 teaspoon

Raisins- 1 tablespoon

Green unsalted pistachio- 1 tablespoon

Black Pepper- ¼ teaspoon, ground coarsely

Method

In a grinder, crush together the almond, cashew nut, poppy seeds, raisins and pistachio.

Place a thick-bottomed wok/pan on your heat source.

Pour in the milk.

When the milk comes to a boil, reduce the heat and keep stirring till the milk is reduced by half.

Add the sugar and the saffron.

Mix well till the sugar is melted and then add the dry fruits that you have crushed in the grinder.

Keep cooking till the mixture gets the consistency of custard.

Switch off the heat source.

Sprinkle the black pepper.

Let the mixture cool and then pour it in to *kulfi* or Popsicle moulds.

Freeze for at least eight hours.

That's all. Your *Dry Fruit Kulfi* is ready.

Prep time: 5 minutes

Cooking time: 30 minutes

Total time: 35 minutes (excluding freezing time)

Kesaria Rabri (Thick Milk Pudding with Saffron)

An easy to make sweet that can be consumed as a grand closure to a great dinner.

Or, paired with hot *jalebis* or *maalpuas*, as some like it.

Serves 3-4

Ingredients

Full cream milk: 2 litres (8 cups)

Milk powder: 1 cup (250 grams)

Sugar- 1 cup (250 grams)

Saffron- about 20 strands dissolved in 2 tablespoon hot milk

Method

Place a thick-bottomed wok/pan on your heat source.

Pour in the milk and add the milk powder.

When the mixture comes to a boil, reduce the heat and keep stirring till the milk is reduced by half.

Add the sugar and the saffron.

Mix well till the sugar is melted and the mixture gets the consistency of custard.

Switch off the heat source.

Let the mixture cool in a fridge.

That's all. Your deliciously rich *Rabri* is ready.

Enjoy cold or with hot *jalebis* or *maalpuas*, if you so wish.

Prep time: 5 minutes

Cooking time: 30 minutes

Total time: 35 minutes

Rabri Fruit Pudding (Thick Milk Pudding with Fruits)

Yet another variation of this great Indian sweet dish.

Serves 3-4

Ingredients

Full cream milk: 2 litres (8 cups)

Milk powder: 1 cup (250 grams)

Sugar- 1 cup (250 grams)

Seasonal cut fruit of your choice- 2 cup (500 grams)

Raisins- 2 tablespoon

Method

Place a thick-bottomed wok/pan on your heat source.

Pour in the milk and add the milk powder.

When the mixture comes to a boil, reduce the heat and keep stirring till the milk is reduced by half.

Add the sugar.

Mix well till the sugar is melted and the mixture gets the consistency of custard.

Switch off the heat source.

When the mixture is cool to touch, add the seasonal cut fruit and raisins.

Let the mixture cool in a fridge.

That's all. Your *Rabri Fruit Pudding* is ready.

Enjoy cold.

Prep time: 15 minutes

Cooking time: 30 minutes

Total time: 45 minutes

Badaam Kheer (Almond Pudding)

Yet another great dish where the goodness of milk protein is enhanced with the goodness of almonds.

Serves 3-4

Ingredients

Full cream milk-1 litre (2 US pints liquid) (4 cups)

Almonds- about 30 blanched and chopped

Sugar to taste - (start with 4 tablespoons)

Milk Powder-2 tablespoons

Green Cardomom-2 crushed

Saffron-few strands (optional)

Method

In a heavy bottomed wok, bring the milk to a boil.

Add the almonds.

Keep stirring on low heat making sure that NOTHING BURNS.

As the mixture begins to thicken, add the milk powder, sugar, the cardamom and the saffron.

Stir well and keep stirring for about 5 minutes.

Switch off the heat source.

That's all.

Your delicious *Badaam Kheer* (Almond Pudding) is ready.

Cool down in the fridge and have it chilled.

Prep time: 5 minute

Cooking time: 20 minutes

Total time: 25 minutes

Chapter 9: Yoghurt as Dessert

"May you eat an unfamiliar dessert in a strange land at least once every three years..."

–Rob Brezsny

It is surprising how frequently yoghurt is used in many Indian dishes. The variety that is used in cooking is cultured yoghurt and is always unflavoured. That way it comes closest to the Greek variety of yoghurt.

Please note that if you buy ready-made yoghurt from the supermarket, sometimes it may splinter when you heat it. This presents an ungainly sight when you are, for example, cooking fish, meat or veggies with yoghurt.

Making Yoghurt at home

If you so desire then, you can very easily make Indian Yoghurt at home using the following method:

First, to start the whole process, you will need to buy some unflavoured yoghurt. Subsequently, about two tablespoons from the yoghurt you make can suffice to make the next home-made batch of yoghurt.

Ingredients

Milk-1 litre (4 cups)

Plain Unsweetened Yoghurt (as starter)-2 tablespoon

Method

Boil the milk well.

Tip: If you don't boil well, your yoghurt will set but will be a little sticky as factory-made yoghurts generally are.

Let the milk cool down to a level where it feels warm but not hot.

You should be able to use your finger for touching the milk without any fear of scalding it.

Beat the yoghurt well and gently add the warm milk.

Mix well.

Now pour this mixture into a bowl and place it in an insulated casserole.

We use an insulated lunch box which has a small heating element built-in. We need to "switch on" this lunch-box for about 30 minutes in really cold weather (where indoor temperatures be below 15 degree C or 59 degree F).

The basic idea is that the milk should remain warm for at least the next three hours.

After that the yoghurt sets on its own.

It is generally advisable to set the yoghurt at night so that you can have fresh yoghurt in the morning. This also ensures that the vessel is not moved during the entire period that the yoghurt is setting because movement spoils the setting.

Prep Time: 5 minutes

Setting Time: 5 hours (minimum three hours)

Shrikhand Mango or Amrakhand (Hung Curd Mango Dessert)

This is a delicacy from Gujrat and Rajasthan from Western India in which hung curd is mixed with sweet mangoes to come up with a simple but irresistible dessert.

Serves 3-4

Ingredients

Ripe Mango–2 (In case fresh mangoes are not available, you can use canned mango pulp. In that case it will be 2 cups or 500 grams of pulp)

Full cream Yoghurt- 1 kg or 1 litre (4 cups approximately)

Castor Sugar – 1 cup (250 grams) if using fresh mangoes; otherwise ½ cup may suffice with sweetened mango pulp.

Fresh cream- 200 grams (1 cup)

Method

Place the full cream yoghurt in a muslin cloth and hang for around four hours to let all the water drip out.

Meanwhile, if using fresh mangoes, remove the skin and also the seed.

Chop the mangoes into small pieces.

In a blender, blend the pieces to make a puree.

Now add the hung curd, cream and the sugar.

Blend well.

Now place the mixture in the fridge for at least two hours so that the *Shrikhand* is chilled well.

That's all. Your delicious Mango *Shrikhand* is ready.

Prep time: 7 minutes (excluding the time to get hung curd)

Cooking time: NIL

Total time: 7 minutes (excluding the time to chill the *Shrikhand* in the fridge)

Shrikhand Kesar (Saffron Hung Curd Dessert)

Yet another hung curd recipe from Western India; this time infused with the goodness and exotic aroma of saffron.

Serves 3-4

Ingredients

Full cream Yoghurt- 1 kg or 1 litre (4 cups approximately)

Castor Sugar – 1 cup (250 grams)

Fresh cream- 200 grams (1 cup)

Saffron- about 20 strands dissolved in 2 tablespoon hot milk

Method

Place the full cream yoghurt in a muslin cloth and hang for around four hours to let all the water drip out.

In a blender, blend together all the ingredients.

Now place the mixture in the fridge for at least two hours so that the *Shrikhand* is chilled well.

That's all. Your delicious *Shrikhand Kesar* is ready.

Prep time: 7 minutes (excluding the time to get hung curd)

Cooking time: NIL

Total time: 7 minutes (excluding the time to chill the *Shrikhand* in the fridge)

Mishti Doi (Sweet Caramel Yoghurt)

This is a classic yoghurt dessert from the Eastern Indian state of West Bengal. Traditionally it is prepared in earthen pots. This ensures a thickish dessert as extra water from the yoghurt keeps on evaporating from the pores of the earthen pot.

Serves 3-4

Ingredients

Full cream milk: 2 litres (8 cups)

Sugar- 1 and a 1/2 cup (375 grams)

Plain Unsweetened Yoghurt (as starter)-4 tablespoon

Method

Boil the milk well.

Tip: If you don't boil well, your yoghurt will set but will be a little sticky as factory-made yoghurts generally are.

While the milk cools down, place another thick-bottomed wok/pan on your heat source and put the sugar for caramelising.

Gently stir till all the sugar melts and gets a golden brown caramelised colour.

Switch off this heat source.

Now pour this molten sugar in to the vessel containing the boiled milk.

BE CAREFUL, BECAUSE THE MILK WILL TEND TO BOIL OVER.

Mix well.

Let the mixture cool down to a level where it feels warm but not hot. That is, you should be able to use your finger for touching the milk without any fear of scalding it.

Beat the yoghurt starter well and gently add to the warm milk.

Mix well.

Now pour this mixture into a bowl and place it in an insulated casserole.

We use an insulated lunch box which has a small heating element built-in. We need to "switch on" this lunch-box for about 30 minutes in really cold weather (where indoor temperatures be below 15 degree C or 59 degree F).

The basic idea is that the milk should remain warm for at least the next four hours.

After that the yoghurt sets on its own.

You may like to set the yoghurt at night. This would ensure that the vessel is not moved during the entire period that the yoghurt is setting because movement spoils the setting.

That's all. Your *Mishti Doi* is ready.

Place it in the fridge for at least two hours so that it is chilled well.

Prep Time: 10 minutes

Setting Time: Minimum four hours

Total time: Approx. six hours (including chilling in the fridge)

Kalakand (A piece of art, literally)

From the West Indian state of Rajasthan, this classic dish presents a clever but delicious mixture of *paneer* and *khoya* that is rare to come by.

Serves 3-4

Ingredients

Full cream milk: 2 litres (8 cups)

Milk powder: 1 cup (250 grams)

Plain Unsweetened Yoghurt -1 cup (250 grams)

Sugar- 1 cup (250 grams)

Saffron: about 20 strands dissolved in 2 tablespoon hot milk

Method

Place a thick-bottomed wok/pan on your heat source.

Pour in the milk.

When the mixture comes to a boil, reduce the heat and keep stirring till the milk is reduced by half.

Add the yoghurt.

Keep stirring till the milk starts curdling a little.

Now add the milk powder, sugar and the saffron.

Mix well till the mixture is almost dry.

Switch off the heat source.

Pour this mixture on to a flat plate.

Let the mixture cool. You can now cut small pieces (in whatever shape you desire) and enjoy.

That's all. Your *Kalakand* is ready.

Prep time: 5 minutes

Cooking time: 35 minutes

Total time: 40 minutes

Mango Lassi (Yoghurt Mango Shake)

Lassis are popular summer coolers from the North Indian state of Punjab that can be served by even wayside eateries (*dhabas*) with aplomb. Sometimes the demand for this drink increases so much that some Punjabi restaurants start using washing machines (in place of household mixers/blenders)!

Serves 3-4

Ingredients

Ripe Mango–2 (In case fresh mangoes are not available, you can use canned mango pulp. In that case it will be 2 cups of pulp)

Yoghurt-500 ml (2 cups approximately)

Crushed ice–200 ml or a cup (Crush the ice before hands in a food processor/or by any other method so that it blends well with the yoghurt).

Sugar, or sugar substitute, to taste

Method

Remove the skin of the mango and also the seed.

Chop the mango into small pieces.

In a blender, blend the pieces.

Now place both the yoghurt and the mangoes in the freezer for about half an hour so that they become really cold.

Blend together the cold yoghurt, the mangoes, sugar and the crushed ice.

Mix well.

In large glasses, pour the blended yoghurt (*Lassi*).

Your delicious Mango *Lassi* is ready.

Prep time: 7 minutes

Cooking time: No cooking time

Total time: 7 minutes

Rose Lassi (Yoghurt Rose Shake)

This is the most popular *Lassi* that you can ask for in any North Indian restaurant.

Serves 3-4

Ingredients

Yoghurt-500 ml (2 cups approximately)

Crushed ice–200 ml or a cup (Crush the ice beforehands in a food processor/or by any other method so that it blends well with the yoghurt).

Sugar, or sugar substitute, to taste

Rose essence- (few drops) or Rose water-1 tablespoon

Method

In a blender, blend together the yoghurt, crushed ice, sugar and rose essence/rose water.

Mix well.

Pour into large glasses.

That's all. Your Rose Flavoured *Lassi* is ready.

Prep time: 2 minutes

Cooking time: No cooking time

Total time: 2 minutes

Chapter 10: The Raj Effect

"Seize the moment. Just think of all those women on the Titanic who said, 'No, thank you,' to dessert that night. And for what!"

–Erma Bombeck

Now we discuss some dishes which have obviously been inspired by the way the British prepared their desserts while ruling over India for almost 200 years. We present just seven such gems here.

Unlike Indian sweetmeats, many of these desserts have no qualms in using eggs. Some of them are also amenable to baking, a technique which is hardly ever used in preparing Indian desserts.

These dishes are now served in India only by some British era clubs. Or by the Indian Armed Forces' messes where British traditions still reign supreme.

N.B. Those looking for an authentic Indian taste, however, may like to skip this chapter.

Caramel Custard

This is a short-cut recipe for this classic dish that uses steaming in place of baking. So, believe it or not, you can, if you so wish, use your ordinary pressure cooker to prepare this recipe.

Serves 3-4

Ingredients

Sweetened Condensed milk-400 grams (1 ½ cup approx.)

Full Cream Milk-3 and half cups

Eggs-5

Vanilla essence–2 drops

Sugar–1/2 cup

Method

Separate the egg yolk and white.

Whisk the white till stiff, then add the egg yolk, and beat the mixture really well.

Mix the milk and the condensed milk well in another vessel.

Now add the beaten egg to the milk and mix well.

Add the vanilla essence.

In a vessel (which should have the capacity to contain the above mixture and which can fit inside a pressure cooker or a steamer), put the sugar and add 2 tablespoon water.

Put it on your heat source, and let the sugar melt.

Switch off the heat the moment the sugar acquires a golden brown colour and immediately add the egg-sugar mixture.

Without stirring, cover the vessel well with one piece of aluminium foil.

Fill the pressure cooker (or steamer) with 3/4th water. In this, immerse the vessel aluminium foil side up to ensure that no water gets into the mixture. Close the pressure cooker's lid without weight/ steamer and turn the heat source on.

When the steam starts escaping (in case of the pressure cooker), reduce the heat to SIM and let it cook for 45 minutes.

If using a steamer, let it steam for 45 minutes.

Thereafter remove the vessel from the cooker/ steamer and let it cool down to room temperature.

Let it then further cool in a fridge for at least 2 hours.

When ready to serve, gently turn the vessel on a plate. Shake slightly and lift the vessel up in one clean movement.

In case, you find the custard not coming out, take a knife and move it on the rim to free the custard from the vessel.

Your beautiful *Caramel Custard* is now ready.

Preparation time: 10 minutes

Cooking time: 50 minutes

Total time: 60 minutes (excluding chilling time in the fridge)

Coconut Cream Caramel

Another variation of the classic dish, but this time infused with the goodness of coconut cream.

Serves 3-4

Ingredients

Sweetened Condensed milk-400 grams (1 ½ cup approx.)

Full Cream Milk-2 cups (500 ml)

Coconut Cream- 1 ½ cups

Eggs-5

Sugar–1/2 cup

Method

Separate the egg yolk and white.

Whisk the white till stiff, then add the egg yolk, and beat the mixture really well.

Mix the milk, coconut cream and the condensed milk well in another vessel.

Now add the beaten egg to the milk and mix well.

In a vessel (which should have the capacity to contain the above mixture and which can fit inside a pressure cooker or a steamer), put the sugar and add 2 tablespoon water.

Put it on your heat source, and let the sugar melt.

Switch off the heat the moment the sugar acquires a golden brown colour and immediately add the egg-sugar mixture.

Without stirring, cover the vessel well with one piece of aluminium foil.

Fill the pressure cooker (or steamer) with 3/4th water. In this, immerse the vessel aluminium foil side up to ensure that no water gets into the mixture. Close the pressure cooker's lid without weight/ steamer and turn the heat source on.

When the steam starts escaping (in case of the pressure cooker), reduce the heat to SIM and let it cook for 45 minutes.

If using a steamer, let it steam for 45 minutes.

Thereafter remove the vessel from the cooker/ steamer and let it cool down to room temperature.

Let it then further cool in a fridge for at least 2 hours.

When ready to serve, gently turn the vessel on a plate. Shake slightly and lift the vessel up in one clean movement.

In case, you find the custard not coming out, take a knife and move it on the rim to free the custard from the vessel.

Your beautiful *Coconut Cream Caramel* is now ready.

Preparation time: 10 minutes

Cooking time: 50 minutes

Total time: 60 minutes (excluding chilling time in the fridge)

Coffee Cream Caramel

Make the same classic dish with coffee if you please.

Serves 3-4

Ingredients

Sweetened Condensed milk-400 grams (1 ½ cup approx.)

Full Cream Milk-3 and half cups

Eggs-5

Vanilla essence–2 drops

Instant Coffee powder- 5 teaspoons

Sugar–1/2 cup

Method

Separate the egg yolk and white.

Whisk the white till stiff, then add the egg yolk, and beat the mixture really well.

Mix the milk, coffee powder, and the condensed milk well in another vessel.

Now add the beaten egg to the milk and mix well.

Add the vanilla essence.

In a vessel (which should have the capacity to contain the above mixture and which can fit inside a pressure cooker or a steamer), put the sugar and add 2 tablespoon water.

Put it on your heat source, and let the sugar melt.

Switch off the heat the moment the sugar acquires a golden brown colour and immediately add the egg-sugar mixture.

Without stirring, cover the vessel well with one piece of aluminium foil.

Fill the pressure cooker (or steamer) with 3/4th water. In this, immerse the vessel aluminium foil side up to ensure that no water gets into the mixture. Close the pressure cooker's lid without weight/ steamer and turn the heat source on.

When the steam starts escaping (in case of the pressure cooker), reduce the heat to SIM and let it cook for 45 minutes.

If using a steamer, let it steam for 45 minutes.

Thereafter remove the vessel from the cooker/ steamer and let it cool down to room temperature.

Let it then further cool in a fridge for at least 2 hours.

When ready to serve, gently turn the vessel on a plate. Shake slightly and lift the vessel up in one clean movement.

In case, you find the custard not coming out, take a knife and move it on the rim to free the custard from the vessel.

Your beautiful *Coffee Cream Caramel* is now ready.

Preparation time: 10 minutes

Cooking time: 50 minutes

Total time: 60 minutes (excluding chilling time in the fridge)

Walnut Praline

This is a take on the classic Indian *chikki* that is prepared with rice flakes or peanuts.

Serves 3-4

Ingredients

Walnut (shelled): 2 cups

Sugar: 1 cup

Ghee (clarified butter) or unsalted butter or cooking oil: 1 teaspoon for greasing the plate

Method

In a thick bottomed wok/pan, add the sugar and put it on your heat source.

As the sugar melts, gently keep stirring.

When the sugar acquires a golden brown colour evenly, switch off the heat source and add the walnuts.

Mix well.

Pour this mixture on to a flat plate lightly greased with *ghee* (clarified butter) or cooking oil.

Let the mixture cool. You can now cut small pieces (in whatever shape you desire) and enjoy.

That's all. Your *Walnut Praline* is ready.

If you wish to store this dish, you can do that in a zip lock or airtight container, without putting in a refrigerator.

Preparation time: 2 minutes

Cooking time: 8 minutes

Total: 10 minutes

Note: You can have endless variation of this recipe by substituting the walnuts with any available nut like peanuts, cashew, almond, etc.

Fruit Pudding

Again a very popular dessert in clubs and Armed Forces' messes in India.

Serves 3-4

Ingredients

Fresh cream -500 ml (1 US pints liquid) (2 cups)

Castor Sugar (to taste) - (start with 3 tablespoon)

Canned fruits-1 cup

Raisins–25 grams (1oz) (1 + 1/2 tablespoon)

Mixed Nuts-50 grams (2oz) (3 tablespoon)

Method

In a bowl, beat the fresh cream and the sugar together.

Add the canned fruits, raisins and nuts.

Mix well. Put the pudding in the fridge and have it when it is chilled. That's all. Your delicious fruit pudding is ready.

Prep time: 10 minutes

Cooking time: NIL

Total time: 10 minutes

Fruit Pudding with Biscuit Base

A variation on the classic dish that does need to be baked.

Serves 3-4

Ingredients

Fresh cream -500 ml (1 US pints liquid) (2 cups)

Castor Sugar (to taste) - (start with 3 tablespoon)

Canned fruits-1 cup

Digestive Biscuits/ cookies – approx. 100 grams (10 pieces)

Butter (salted) – 2 tablespoon

Method

In a blender, crush the digestive biscuits well.

Now add butter and blend well.

In a baking dish, spread this mixture and put it in a pre-heated oven.

Bake for 10 minutes at 180 degree Celsius (356 degree Fahrenheit).

Remove from the oven and let it cool down.

In a bowl, beat the fresh cream and the sugar together.

Add the canned fruits.

Mix well.

Pour this mixture over the baked biscuits.

Put the pudding in the fridge and have it when it is chilled.

That's all. Your delicious *Fruit Pudding with Biscuit Base* is ready.

Prep time: 10 minutes

Cooking time: 10 minute (excluding pre-heat time)

Total time: 20 minutes

Custard Pudding Indian Style WITHOUT EGGS

When you have less time or don't have the patience to bake/steam a custard dish, this is an alternative you can try for turning out a delicious fruit pudding. Once again, this is a very popular dish at the messes of Indian military or para-military forces.

Serves 3-4

Ingredients

Full cream milk-1 litre (2 US pints liquid) (4 cups)

Sugar (to taste) - (start with 3 tablespoon)

Corn Flour-3 tablespoon

Vanilla/Orange essence-3 drops

Chopped fresh seasonal fruits-1 cup

Raisins–25 grams (1oz) (1 + 1/2 tablespoon)

Mixed Nuts-50 grams (2oz) (3 tablespoon)

Method

Dissolve the corn flour in ½ cup milk.

In a heavy bottomed wok, bring the rest of the milk to boil.

Add the dissolved corn flour to the milk.

The milk will immediately start getting a thick consistency.

Switch off the heat source.

When the mixture cools a little, add the fresh fruits, raisins, nuts and the essence.

Let it cool down and then put the pudding in the fridge.

Have it when it is cold.

Prep time: 5 minutes

Cooking time: 5 minutes

Total time: 10 minutes

A Big Thank You for Reading This Book till the End

I'm indeed grateful that you chose MY BOOK.

I know you could have easily picked up any other book in this genre but am glad that you took a chance with mine.

So a big THANKS for reposing your trust in me and reading this book all the way to the end.

If you liked this book, I shall be grateful if you could do me a small favour.

Please take a moment to leave a review, on the eBook platform you bought it on, if you are happy.

If not, please tell me directly. Your feedback is of immense value to me as an Author.

Your suggestions will help me in writing the kind of books that you love.

Books by the Author in the "Cooking In A Jiffy" Series

HOME STYLE INDIAN COOKING IN A JIFFY

(Now available also in Italian, Japanese and Spanish)

Amazon #1 Best Seller in Indian and Professional Cooking

With an amazing compilation of over 100 delectable Indian dishes, many of which you can't get in any Indian restaurant for love or for money, this is unlike any other Indian Cook book.

What this book focuses on is what Indians eat every day in their homes.

It then in a step-by-step manner makes this mysterious, never disclosed, "Home Style" Indian cooking accessible to anyone with a rudimentary knowledge of cooking and a stomach for adventure.

HOW TO COOK IN A JIFFY EVEN IF YOU HAVE NEVER BOILED AN EGG BEFORE

(Now available also in Italian, German and Portuguese)

Never boiled an egg before but want to learn the magic art of cooking?

Then don't leave home without this Survival Cookbook.

Be it healthy college cooking, or cooking for a single person or even outdoor cooking—this book helps you survive all situations by teaching you how to cook, literally in a JIFFY.

Where this book scores over other how to cookbooks is the structured manner in which it follows a step by step "graduation" process. You start with some very basic cooking techniques such as how to break, boil and peel an egg, learn how to handle chicken, vegetables and fish and then "graduate" to making such "complicated" recipes as cheese omelette, vegetables au gratin, baked chicken or French Onion Soup.

Most uniquely, the book teaches the concept of "sequencing and parallel processing" in cooking to enable busy people to create a 3-4 course meal in less than 30 minutes.

The book is fun and entertaining to read with the author sharing his own personal story of bumbling about in the wonderlands of cooking, with wit and humour.

HEALTHY COOKING IN A JIFFY: THE COMPLETE NO FAD NO DIET HANDBOOK

(Now available also in Portuguese and Spanish)

Amazon #1 in Hot New Releases in Health, Fitness & Dieting> Special Diets> Healthy

Amazon #3 Best Seller in Health, Fitness & Dieting> Special Diets> Healthy

A Complete No Fad No Diet No Nonsense Handbook for Healthy Cooking And That Too In A Jiffy

If you have ever wondered how you can be healthy without dieting, following any peculiar fads, eating any esoteric foods, injecting any hormones or downing any pills, potions or supplements, you have come absolutely to the right place.

In that background, the book presents a veritable cornucopia of easy recipes to give you an idea of what you can cook to achieve your target of having regularly a balanced diet.

You will find ideas on how to cook your vegetables in a simple and tasty manner, how to handle pasta recipes, chicken recipes, fish recipes, mutton recipes, milk shakes (even if you hate drinking plain milk), breakfast recipes, lunch and dinner recipes and some

Asian recipes when you feel the need to have something different and exciting.

So if you are sick of dieting, counting calories, or gorging on supplements, do consider investing in this book of simply sensible cooking and get on to a journey of eternal joy and happiness.

THE ULTIMATE GUIDE TO COOKING LENTILS THE INDIAN WAY

(Now available also in German)

Amazon #1 Best Seller in Indian Cooking and Rice & Grains

Presenting 58 Tastiest Ways to Cook Lentils as Soups, Curries, Snacks, Full Meals and hold your breath, Desserts! As only Indians can.

So say bye to boring lentil salads or sickening canned baked beans, and open your mind to the bewildering ways that Indians employ to let lentils form a part of every meal that they have, as dal (soup), curry, snack or even dessert.

"The Ultimate Guide to Cooking Lentils the Indian Way" lets you savour, in this background, as many as twenty most popular "Home Style" dal recipes; ten curries; six lentil dishes cooked with rice; eleven snacks; three kebabs; three lentil stuffed parathas; and five desserts.

This could simply be the ultimate vegetarian protein cookbook you can possess.

THE ULTIMATE GUIDE TO COOKING RICE THE INDIAN WAY

Amazon #1 in Hot New Releases in Rice & Grains

From a Bed for Curries, to *Pilaf, Biryani, Khichdi, Idli, Dosa*, Savouries and Desserts, No One Cooks Rice as Lovingly as the Indians Do.

From Prasenjeet Kumar, the Amazon #1 bestseller of the "Cooking In A Jiffy" series of books, comes the ultimate rice cookbook that anyone looking for gluten-free food should just grab with both hands.

Cataloguing the legendary "love affair" that Indians have with rice, the book narrates how rice forms an intrinsic part of every Indian's life from birth till death.

In this background, this rice cookbook presents a total of 35 mouth-watering rice dishes, including 20 dishes where rice cookers can be used.

There are eight plain rice recipes, five for cooking rice with lentils, five each for cooking rice with vegetables and meats, five ways to use rice in snacks and seven as desserts.

THE ULTIMATE GUIDE TO COOKING FISH THE INDIAN WAY

43 Mouth-watering Ways to Cooking Fish in a JIFFY as Only Indians Can.

From Prasenjeet Kumar, the #1 best-selling author of the "Cooking In A Jiffy" series of cookbooks, comes the Ultimate Guide to Cooking Fish with such exotic spices and taste that you will be left asking for more.

So say bye to the boring boiled and broiled ways to make fish and prawn dishes and let this new book open your eyes to the wonderful possibilities of cooking fish the way northern, southern, eastern and western Indians do.

There are six starter (or dry) dishes, 14 curries, 12 prawn dishes, and 4 ways to cook fish head and eggs (caviar) the Indian way.

For the spice-challenged or nostalgia ridden folks, there are 7 dishes from the days of the British Raj.

So if you were wondering how to incorporate this superb, dripping with long strands of polyunsaturated essential omega-3 fatty acids (that the human body can't naturally produce), low-calorie, high quality protein rich white meat in your daily diet, just grab this book with both your hands.

THE ULTIMATE GUIDE TO COOKING CHICKEN THE INDIAN WAY

51 mouth-watering "Home-Style" ways to cooking chicken in a JIFFY as only Indians Can

From Prasenjeet Kumar, the #1 best-selling author of the "Cooking In A Jiffy" series of cookbooks, comes the absolutely Ultimate Guide to Cooking Chicken with such exotic spices and taste that you will be left asking for more.

You will learn to cook chicken with yoghurt and coconut milk, mustard and turmeric, curry leaves and *garam masala* (literally hot spices) and so on.

There are 7 starter (or snack) dishes, 8 dry recipes, 15 chicken curries, 5 recipes for cooking chicken with rice, and 8 ways to cook eggs THE INDIAN WAY.

For the spice-challenged or nostalgia ridden folks, there are 8 dishes from the days of the British Raj that do use cheese and involve baking, if you were missing that!

And the bottom line is that you master these and you can handle any Indian non-vegetarian dish, the author promises.

So if you were till now wondering how to incorporate this superb, low-calorie, high quality protein rich white meat in your daily diet in the tastiest manner possible, just grab this book with both your hands.

THE ULTIMATE GUIDE TO COOKING VEGETABLES THE INDIAN WAY

101 Tastiest Ways to Cook Veggies as Snacks, Soups, Curries, Full Meals and hold your breath, Desserts! As only Indians can.

From the author of # 1 Best seller "Cooking In A Jiffy" series of cookbooks, comes a tribute to vegetables, the way Indians cook them in their homes.

So forget your boring boiled and broiled and baked ways to make veggie dishes and let this new book open your eyes to the wonderful possibilities of cooking vegetables the way northern, southern, eastern and western Indians do.

"The Ultimate Guide to Cooking Vegetables the Indian Way" lets you savour, in this background, as many as twenty-six most popular "Home Style" curries, 24 dry recipes, 10 recipes for cooking veggies with rice or breads, and 19 kinds of snacks and accompaniments. Most recipes are low-calorie and with OPTIONAL use of chillies.

For the spice-challenged or nostalgia ridden folks, there are 14 dishes from the days of the British Raj that do use cheese and involve baking, if you were missing that!

Finally there are 8 desserts Indians love to make from veggies.

And the bottom line is that you master these and you can handle any Indian vegetable dish from any part of India, we promise.

Books by the Author in the Romance Genre

LEGALLY IN LOVE (Book 1 in the Romance in India Series)

Meet Amit Verma, a 27 year-old dreamy corporate lawyer looking for a job in Delhi, India.

One morning, while going through his mobile phone contact list, he comes across the entry for Naina Karnad, a girl who stole his heart some two years back in his former workplace.

The problem: He has not dialled her number in a year.

Will they ever meet again?

Will their love life survive the corporate intrigues and the recession?

"Legally in love" is a powerful tale of two souls battling their way through the ruthless world of corporate office politics to discovering their true love and passion.

LOVE KARMA CROSSED (Book 2 in Romance in India Series)

He vowed he'd love her so much that even death will be scared to come near her.....

MUMBAI: Raj Sharma, an aspiring Bollywood actor, is devastated when he learns that his wife, Nisha, a celebrity singer and a woman he deeply loves, is terminally ill.

Nobody can save her.

Not modern or ancient medicine.

Not prayers or religious mumbo-jumbo.

Not soothsayers or evil eye totems—nothing works.

Raj believes only his love can save Nisha.

Others think that is irrational stupidity.

Who is right?

Will Raj succeed?

Or will the inevitable happen?

And will Raj be forced to helplessly watch his lovely wife die bit by bit in front of his eyes?

Strangely Raj and Nisha decide to embark on a journey. A life changing journey.

From the glittering lights of Hong Kong to the intriguing caves, ruins, churches and mosques of Turkey, the journey unravels the deepest mysteries of the human heart.

And always posing the question—whether love can really heal?

WHEN GANGES MET THE NORTH SEA

From Prasenjeet Kumar, the Amazon # 1 Best-selling Author, comes a romantic tale of how two lives, one from India and the other from Sweden, converge in London in the most unexpected and shocking of ways.

DELHI: Meet Anuj Kaul, a twenty something college student.

Inspired by his Cousin Nisha Sharma's love story, he longs to find his true love someday.

But his romantic liaisons disappoint him so much that he vows never to fall in love again.

LONDON: Ella Akerson, a London Royal College of Music student and a brilliant violinist, is on the verge of dying.

Her problem: She is her own worst enemy.

Anuj and Ella. Two souls like two rivers meet in London.

Different origins. One destination—True ever-lasting love.

Will Anuj find true love?

And can love save Ella from the path of self-destruction she has herself embarked on?

Books by the Author in the "Quiet Phoenix" Series

CELEBRATING QUIET PEOPLE: UPLIFTING STORIES FOR INTROVERTS AND HIGHLY SENSITIVE PERSONS

(Now available also in French, Italian, Portuguese, and Spanish.)

Celebrating Quiet People: A unique collection of motivational, inspirational and uplifting TRUE stories for introverts and highly sensitive persons that you shouldn't miss....

From the Amazon #1 best-selling author of the "Quiet Phoenix" series of books comes an outstanding collection of biographies and events that guarantee to increase your self-compassion and self-esteem, regardless of your age, gender or status in society.

QUIET PHOENIX: AN INTROVERT'S GUIDE TO RISING IN CAREER & LIFE

(Now available also in Italian and Spanish.)

Amazon #1 Best Seller in Legal Profession and Ethics & Professional Responsibility

Like the legendary Phoenix bird rising from the ashes, "Quiet Phoenix" is an incredible career change story that Prasenjeet Kumar shares, with wit and charm, of the journey from being a Corporate Lawyer to becoming a Full Time Author-Entrepreneur using his introversion as a strength to overcome all obstacles.

QUIET PHOENIX 2: FROM FAILURE TO FULFILMENT: A MEMOIR OF AN INTROVERTED CHILD

(Now available also in Japanese and Portuguese)

Amazon #1 Hot New Releases in Biographies & Memoirs > Professional and Academics > Educators

Celebrating The Quiet Child: A Must Read For every Parent, Teacher, Mentor, Sports Coach.........

Based on the author's own childhood experiences, the underlying theme of the book is that your Quiet Child is built for persistence, creativity, and self-discipline. She will also, without any goading, display a knack for self-learning, high emotional intelligence and an impeccable sense of moral responsibility. So nurture and celebrate that Quiet Child.

CELEBRATING QUIET LEADERS: UPLIFTING STORIES OF INTROVERTED LEADERS WHO CHANGED HISTORY

(Now available also in Portuguese and Spanish)

What do you think is common between George Washington and the Buddha, Mustafa Kemal Atatürk and Nelson Mandela, Rosa Parks and Florence Nightingale.........

That they were great leaders?

True. But did you know that they were also all introverts?

From Prasenjeet Kumar, the Amazon #1 best-selling author, comes an outstanding collection of uplifting stories of the greatest leaders of all times that have used their powers of introversion to rewrite History.

Most importantly, these leaders succeeded not because they could overcome their introversion, BUT because of their gifted strengths of introversion.

So, ladies and gentlemen, be prepared to immerse yourselves into legendary tales of courage and valour shown by quiet, shy and sensitive men and women from all around the world.

CELEBRATING QUIET ARTISTS: STIRRING STORIES OF INTROVERTED ARTISTS WHO THE WORLD CAN'T FORGET

Finally a Book that Celebrates the Creativity and Rich Imagination of Introverts

Do you really think legends like Steven Spielberg, Agatha Christie, J.K. Rowling, Leonardo Da Vinci, Amitabh Bachchan and the like were extroverted and outgoing— unlike you?

No. Absolutely wrong.

They were quiet. And introverts. Like me. Like you. And yet, their contribution is so well known.

Just imagine a world WITHOUT them. What would it be like? Without Harry Potter. Without Mona Lisa. Without Hercule Poirot. Without Inspector Vijay. Without E.T.

So if these artists were really introverts like you and me, how did they leave such an indelible imprint on this world?

Did they learn to fake extroversion? Did they practise skills of socialising? Did they learn to talk non-stop?

Hell no.

They stayed true to themselves.

Puzzled? Then grab a copy today!

And enjoy many refreshing stories of introverted artists who used their god gifted strengths of introversion to overcome heart-breaking tragedies, challenges, and setbacks.

Books by the Author in the "Self-Publishing WITHOUT SPENDING A DIME" Series

HOW TO BE AN AUTHOR ENTREPRENEUR WITHOUT SPENDING A DIME

(Now Available also in Spanish and Italian)

Are you making the same costly mistakes that Authors usually make?

If that be so, then here is a book that can help realize your author-entrepreneur dreams WITHOUT SPENDING A DIME.

This book contains everything you need to know about self-publishing and also contains a list of helpful video tutorials and resources.

HOW TO TRANSLATE YOUR BOOKS WITHOUT SPENDING A DIME

(Now Available also in Portuguese and Italian)

Enca$h the power of translation WITHOUT SPENDING A DIME.

Remember Paulo Coelho's "The Alchemist"? Could it be setting a Guinness World Record if it had not sold more than 65 million copies in 67 different languages?

So if you too could translate your bestseller FROM ENGLISH INTO DIFFERENT WORLD LANGUAGES, it could mean reaching such newer, untapped, unexplored markets whose existence you were blissfully unaware of.

Interested? Then grab this DIY manual of practical tips and advice that can take your writing dreams to literally translation Nirvana.

HOW TO MARKET YOUR BOOKS WITHOUT SPENDING A DIME

(Also available in Italian)

Finally a Book on Marketing that cuts out the Fluff and Focuses only on the ESSENTIALS.

Are you bombarded with strange and esoteric marketing advice, to sell your books in 1000 ways, that leaves you baffled, bewildered and terribly confused?

Do you feel that learning and mastering those complicated strategies have sucked away all the joy you once had for writing?

Then this book focusing on the BARE ESSENTIALS for marketing your book may just be what the doctor ordered.

From Prasenjeet Kumar, the Amazon #1 Best Selling Author of "Self-Publishing WITHOUT SPENDING A DIME" series of books, comes a book that after discussing all the fluff and jargon that marketing gurus spout establishes why

less is always more."

At last!

Connect With the Authors

Feel free to visit us at:

http://www.cookinginajiffy.com

Should you have any questions or comments, or desire to collaborate with us on any future project, please do not hesitate to write to us anytime at ciaj@cookinginajiffy.com.

We are definitely looking for partners for carrying the "Cooking In A JIFFY" series forward to cover it by national/regional cuisines.

So if you are game to do, say "Home Style German/Italian/Chinese/Japanese.... Cooking In A JIFFY" with us, do please get in touch.

We would also love to connect with you on Social Media. Join us on:

Twitter

https://twitter.com/CookinginaJiffy

Goodreads

https://www.goodreads.com/prasenjeet

Google Plus

https://www.google.com/+PrasenjeetKumarAuthor

About The Authors

Prasenjeet Kumar

Prasenjeet Kumar is the author of over 21 books in four genres: Fiction-Romance, motivational books for introverts (the Quiet Phoenix series), books on Self-Publishing (Self-Publishing Without Spending a Dime series) and cookbooks (Cooking In A Jiffy series). His books (25 titles so far) have also been translated into French, German, Italian, Japanese, Spanish, and Portuguese.

Prasenjeet is a Law graduate from the University College London (2005-2008), London University and a Philosophy Honours graduate from St. Stephen's College (2002-2005), Delhi University. In addition, he holds a Legal Practice Course (LPC) Diploma from College of Law, Bloomsbury, London.

Prasenjeet loves gourmet food, music, films, golf and travelling. He has already covered seventeen countries including Canada, China, Denmark, Dubai, Germany, Hong Kong, Indonesia, Macau, Malaysia, Sharjah, Sweden, Switzerland, Thailand, Turkey, UK, Uzbekistan, and the USA.

Prasenjeet is the self-taught designer, writer, editor and proud owner of the website cookinginajiffy.com which he has dedicated to his mother. He also runs another website publishwithprasen.com where he shares tips about writing and self-publishing.

Sonali Kumar

Sonali Kumar retired from the Indian Administrative Service (IAS) after a distinguished service of over 36 years with the Government of India as well as the Government of Jammu and Kashmir.

During this period, she held a number of assignments related to industry and commerce (including Public Sector Undertakings), textiles (handlooms & handicrafts), education, welfare, forests & environment, agriculture, horticulture, co-operatives, rural and urban development, health & medical education, anti-drought prone and anti-desert area development programmes, revenue, judicial, and even disaster relief operations.

Sonali believes that her myriad experiences spanning all kinds of sectors have equipped her with the powers of ideation, problem-solving, out-of-box thinking, and strategic policy insights that only a long stint in IAS probably can endow one with.

Post-retirement, Sonali is working with her son Prasenjeet putting out books in the "Cooking In A Jiffy" series. In her spare time, she doesn't mind mentoring or advising people who wish to benefit from her otherwise vast experience in public service.

Index